BUDAPEST

Part of the Langenscheidt Publishing Group

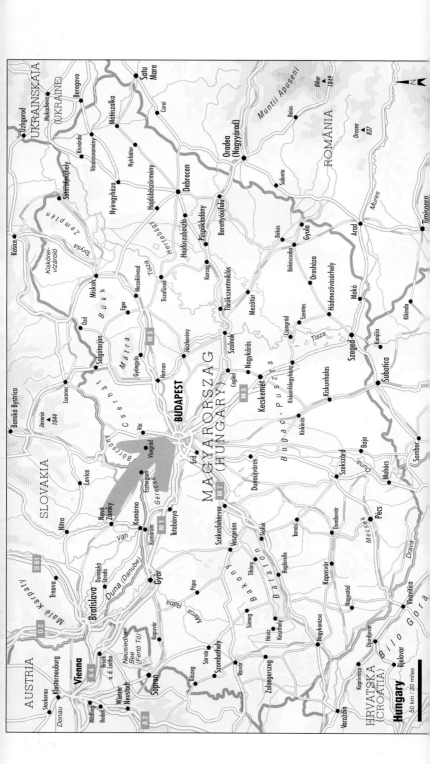

Welcome

his guidebook combines the interests and enthusiasms of two of the world's best-known information providers: Insight Guides, who have set the standard for visual travel guides since 1970, and Discovery Channel, the world's premier source of non-fiction television programming. Its aim is to bring you the best of the Hungarian capital and its surroundings in a series of tailor-made itineraries originally conceived by Alfred Horn, with the help of Zoltan Ivanij, a native of Budapest.

This book shows visitors how to make best use of a short stay in the city. Three full-day itineraries deal with the three key areas: the castle quarter of Buda, the centre of Pest and along the River Danube. These are followed by nine itineraries focusing on other interesting areas and aspects of the city, plus three easy excursions. The back section of the guide offers ideas on eating out, shopping, nightlife and festivals, and the Practical Information section provides a wealth of useful travel tips.

Alfred Horn's interest in Budapest developed in the 1960s when he began making regular visits from his native Germany. He was especially impressed by its atmosphere of prosperity, which he found in marked contrast to other East European capitals. Here, East meets West and the past is always present. The glory days of the Austro-Hungarian Empire are nostalgically recalled by the city's fine architecture, plush coffee houses and passion for operetta, and Ottoman influences are alive and well in the spicy cuisine and Turkish baths.

This edition of the guide has been substantially revised and expanded by the writer and editor **Marcus Brooke**, who travelled to Budapest to road-test and update the original tours, add new excursions, and write new sections on eating out and nightlife. A regular traveller and contributor to the Insight Guides series, Marcus Brooke has a special interest in the cities of Central Europe.

HISTORY AND CULTURE

CITY ITINERARIES

The first three full-day itineraries combine the great attractions of the city's three key areas. Nine further itineraries explore other interesting aspects and areas of the city.

contents

Pages 2/3: the Parliament building
Pages 8/9: playing chess at Széchenyi thermal baths

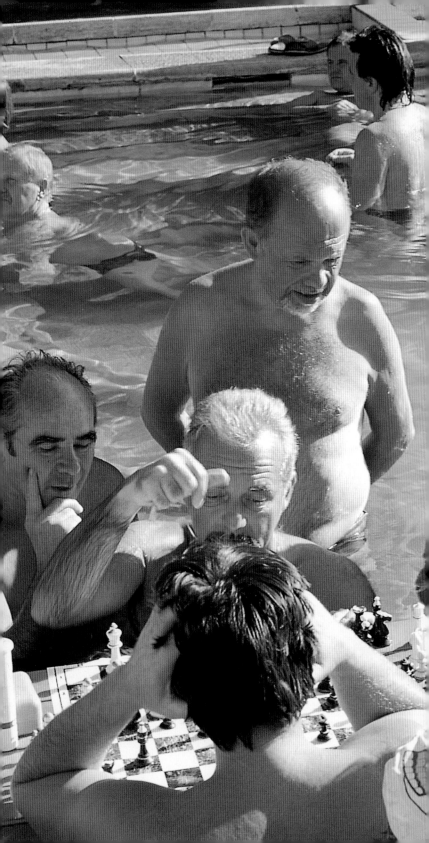

History & *Culture*

n the mid-1st century BC, the Celtic Eravisci tribe, attracted by a ford in the Danube, was settling in what is now the Budapest area. Its 'ample water' informed its first name: *Ak-Ink*. This became Aquincum a century later when the Romans built a military camp on the site. The town that sprang up was granted the status of a *colonia* by Emperor Septimius Severus in AD198. But as the Roman Empire began to decline, so did the capital of the Roman province of Pannonia (west Hungary). Attila the Hun and his brother Bleda established a presence in Aquincum around AD 450. The Avars, a nomadic people from the steppes of Asia, then controlled the region, with Slavonic tribes started to arrive in the 6th century.

In the 9th century the nomadic Magyars appeared on the Pannonian plain. After a few vain attempts to advance further west, the Hungarians-to-be contented themselves with the middle basin of the Danube. Their king, Stephen I (1000–1038, later St Stephen) adopted the Christian faith, and his wife, Gisela, invited German immigrants to the country. New towns sprang up, and the rulers of the house of Árpád chose Esztergom, on the knee of the Danube, as their capital. The settlement of Pest on the east bank was founded by Slavs.

Mongol Invasion

In 1241 the Mongols, distant relatives of the Huns, overran the country and destroyed all the settlements that stood on the city's present-day site. The terrified population fled to the long, rocky plateau of limestone cliffs above the western bank of the Danube, where they built a fortress. Before long the improvised refuge became a town in its own right. The Hungarians called it Buda, after the first constable of the Castle Hill fortress; the Germans, who constituted a majority here from the 13th to 16th centuries, knew it as Ofen. What had been Aquincum now became Óbuda (Old Buda). Pest was rebuilt during the reign of King Béla IV, and the Golden Bull of 1244 granted it full civic privileges. Development, however, concentrated on Buda. In 1276 King Ladislas IV granted it civic rights, and in the mid-14th century the Angevin kings set up court here.

The Hungarians' minority status in Buda was reinforced by the arrival of numerous Jews, Serbs and Germans. Only in the 15th century did Hungarians form more than half the membership of the city council. Buda's ethnic mix was conducive to industrial and cultural prosperity. After the defeat of Prague during the Hussite Wars, Buda developed into a full-blown European metropolis under King Sigismund, who went on to be elected king of Germany in 1410 and later Holy Roman Emperor. Under the humanist rule of King Mátyás

Left: St Stephen guards the Fishermen's Bastion
Right: the 10th-century Magyar leader Lehel probably blew this ivory horn

The Turul

High up on Budapest's Freedom Bridge (Szabadság híd), a huge bird can be seen spreading its wings. This is the *turul*, half-eagle and half-vulture, which is the totem of the Magyars. In their ancient lands – the steppes between the Volga River and the Urals – the bird brought them luck because it showed the way to fresh pasture land, and its scream warned them when enemies were approaching. For the traditional shaman, or *táltos*, the bird was a source of wise advice. It thus accompanied the tribes on their wanderings as far as the Danube basin, eventually to become the mystical symbol of history-conscious Hungary. On house facades and mountain peaks, sculpted from stone or cast in bronze, the *turul* stands guard over city and country.

Corvinus (1458–90), the city thrived politically and become a focal point of Western learning and culture.

However, following Suleiman's accession as sultan in 1520, the Turks conquered Hungary at the Battle of Molhács in 1526. Pozsony (today's Bratislava) became the capital of what was left of Hungary while a Turkish pasha ruled in Buda, which became a prosperous provincial capital within the Ottoman Empire. The Turks fostered a sense of community and, although some churches were turned into mosques, Christians and Jews were allowed to practise their religion. But Germans were expelled from the city as the Turks continued to do battle with the Habsburgs. The most visible legacy of the Ottoman Empire in Budapest today are the Turkish baths.

The Christians' recapture of the city was such a bloody affair that Buda had to be founded again, while the settlements around the city had to wait decades for attention. Buda's royal buildings, churches and houses nearly all date from the 18th century, though most were built on medieval foundations. Only in 1703 did Buda and Pest finally regain the status of free imperial cities.

The Greatest Hungarian

The Habsburgs reigning in Vienna donned the crown of St Stephen and ruled with an iron fist. The local population rebelled against their erstwhile liberators, whom they fought from 1703 to 1711 under the Transylvanian Ferenc II Rákóczi. Eventually Rákóczi's allies abandoned him and he went into self-imposed exile in Turkey, where he died in 1735. The Habsburgs became more tolerant, and the second quarter of the century saw the appearance of the Reform Movement led by the liberal Count István Széchenyi – 'The Greatest Hungarian'. He did his best to lead Hungary to autonomy through political compromises with the Austrians, and he was the first to call for the union of Buda and Pest. He may have failed but he left lasting legacies such as the Academy of Sciences, the Chain Bridge, the widening of the Danube and Tsiz, and the construction of railways and roads. And he introduced English thoroughbred horses – ancestors of today's *puszta* horses.

The radical Lajos Kossuth led another

Right: a fine Turkish figure on a facade

uprising in 1848, which the Habsburgs crushed with the help of Russian troops. The Habsburgs secured their hold on the city by building the citadel on Gellérthegy. In 1867, under the Austrian foreign minister and later Reich chancellor Count von Beust, the Austro-Hungarian Compromise formed the basis for the Austro-Hungarian monarchy. The crown of St Stephen was still worn by a Habsburg, but the Hungarians had autonomy. This freedom was soon exploited to 'magyarise' Slovakia, a region still happily referred to in Budapest as the 'Upper Country'. Most of today's problems between Hungary and Slovakia have roots in this historical development.

Buda, Pest and the town of Óbuda (north of Buda) were united in 1872 and Budapest was declared a royal capital in 1893. Traffic congestion was eased after the construction of the inner and outer ring-roads and major radial streets such as the Andrássy út. The first underground railway in continental Europe, today's M1, was built in this period. In 1903 the impressive Elisabeth Bridge was built. The architecture of these years of industrial expansion is a distinctive feature of today's city centre. The Opera House, Parliament Building, Hotel Astoria, Vigadó concert hall and numerous coffee houses bear witness to the city's prosperity at the dawn of the 20th century.

The Spoils of Defeat

In 1918 Hungary found itself on the losing side of World War I. The governing National Council soon collapsed, as did the soviet republic under Béla Kun that had replaced it. In 1919, Admiral Horthy and his 'national army' seized power, but they could do little to prevent 1920's Treaty of Trianon depriving the country of three-fifths of its land: Slovakia was incorporated into Czechoslovakia, Transylvania was given to Romania, Croatia to Yugoslavia. Budapest was overrun by thousands of refugees from these territories.

Industrial production returned to its prewar level, and public construction projects alleviated homelessness and unemployment, but in its foreign policy, Hungary backed the wrong horse, again. Hoping to win back the territories it had lost, it formed alliances with fascist Italy and Nazi Germany.

Above: Pozsony, now Bratislava, took over Buda's administrative role in 1526

When, in October 1944, Horthy attempted to free Hungary from German tutelage, he was imprisoned, and the Nazis called on the fascist Nyilaskeresztes Párt (Arrow Cross Party) to form a puppet government. This resulted in a traumatic end to the war for Hungary, especially for its Jewish population. At the end of the 19th century, around a quarter of Budapest's population was Jewish, and their genocide would have been all the more complete were it not for the heroic efforts of the Swedish diplomat Raoul Wallenberg. Meanwhile Budapest was severely damaged as the Soviet Red Army inexorably moved in on the Wehrmacht, which held out until February 1945.

Communist Control

In November 1945, in the first free elections to be held for many decades, the Smallholders Party, with its social reform programme, won 57 percent of the vote and a republic was declared in February 1946. But the communists had gained control of the police force and, with the support of the Red Army, they seized power in 1949. Stalin's henchman Mátyás Rákosi liquidated his critics within the party and led Hungary to socialist tragedy.

In 1956, led by Imre Nagy and supported by the army, Budapest rebelled. Soviet troops crushed the uprising in days. Thousands died, and Nagy and his acolytes were executed after a show-trial in 1958. János Kádár was left with the task of administering the political and social mess that remained. He showed loyalty to the Soviet Union by sending two Hungarian divisions to Czechoslovakia in 1968 to end the 'Prague Spring', but at home he started loosening the reins. His 'goulash communism' revitalised the economy and generated a degree of scientific and artistic freedom unknown in the Eastern bloc. Indeed the first tear in the Iron Curtain appeared in Hungary – in 1989, when the new reformist communist government allowed thousands of refugees from the former East Germany to escape to the West.

In 1990 Hungary elected a radical conservative government that privatised industry but at a cost of high inflation and unemployment. In 1994 the

Above: a moment of short-lived hope before the 1956 uprising was crushed

reformed socialists, led by Gyula Horn, returned to power, but the administration was plagued by corruption; four years later the Fidesz-Hungarian Civic Party led by Viktor Orbán formed a coalition government.

Cultural Influences

Hungary has been part of Western Europe since it adopted Christianity as its state religion around 1000, but it has always been a cultural outsider. The language is esoteric, and a uniform national identity depends on the relatively small number of Magyars. Even during the reign of St Stephen, foreigners were invited to settle the country. For a long time the idea of a Hungarian national culture was not entertained seriously outside the country, and even today Hungary's image abroad is still associated with gypsy romance, operettas by Franz Lehár and genuine Hungarian salami.

This image does not reflect the reality: gypsies are not Magyars at all – they probably came from Sind in present-day Pakistan. It was only *circa* 1500 that reports began to arrive from Buda about 'lute-playing gypsies from Egypt'. And Lehár, born in 1870 in the border town of Komárom, was mostly successful in Vienna, and died in the Austrian town of Bad Ischl. Even the recipe for Hungarian salami came from Verona.

Yet Hungarian culture is alive and well. Hungarians have always been open to outside influences, blending widely differing ethnic elements and cultural trends into an entirely new synthesis. The poetry of the early Magyars was handed down through oral traditions and thus survives in the country's myths and legends. A funeral oration from the dawn of the 13th century is the oldest surviving source of medieval Hungarian. The earliest Hungarian writers, such as János Pannonius, the Bishop of Pécs (1434–72), wrote in Latin. It was only as a result of the Hussite (Czech) influence that the Bible was first translated into Hungarian at the beginning of the 15th century.

In the centuries that followed this milestone, the written language was further refined by translators such as János Sylvester and Gáspár Károlyi as well as by the gradual appearance in print of Hungarian grammars and Latin-Hungarian dictionaries. Bálint Balassi (1554–94), the first poet to write in popular Hungarian, developed his own style and verse form in a series of highly expressive songs of love and war.

Popular elements such as the *verbunkos*, a traditional dance associated with the recruitment of soldiers, was central to the genesis of 'typically Hungarian' music, which was further developed in the 18th century by violin virtuosi such as János Bihari and Anton Csermák. This is where Hungarian gypsy music, distinctive for its long introductions *(Lassú)* followed by fast, syncopated dance sections *(Friss)*, has its roots. Franz Liszt (1811–86) left his native Hungary as a child prodigy, achieving success in the Paris salons and

Right: the Red Army's liberation on 4 April 1945 soon gave way to communist oppression

as director of music in Weimar before settling in Budapest and becoming president of the Academy of Music. Liszt considered this music to be 'originally Hungarian' and used it as the basis of his *Hungarian Rhapsodies*. His spiritual disciple Béla Bartók (1881–1945) taught at the Academy of Music in Budapest before emigrating to New York in 1940. With Zoltán Kodály, he collected more than 6,000 Magyar, Slovakian and Romanian folk melodies, and added their elemental rhythms to many of his works.

Hungarian literature of the 19th century went the same way, from Romantic to Modern. Ferenc Kölcsey (1790–1838), who wrote the national anthem, and Mihály Vörösmarty (1800–55), whose monument in Pest is inscribed with his *Ode to the Fatherland*, were models for the patriotic revolutionaries of 1848. Sándor Petőfi (1823–49), whose democratic verses were admired throughout Europe, became the revolutionaries' symbolic martyr, and the popular folk hero *Toldi*, created by János Arany, became their literary myth.

Imre Madách (1823–64), the country's greatest classical dramatist, is best known for his poetic drama *The Tragedy of Man*, in which his protagonist, Adam, is on the verge of despair when confronted with a version of mankind's possible future. While the brilliant and prolific novelist Mór Jókai (1823–1904) was enjoying success with his romances, Kálmán Mikszath (1847–1910) became a master of ironic social criticism, a genre which later featured prominently in the works of Zsigmond Móricz (1879–1942). The literary periodical *Nyugat* ('The West') had a decisive influence on literary life in Hungary from 1908 to 1941. In her novel *Stations*, in which she elevated the emancipation of women to a literary theme, Margit Kaffka (1880–1918) described the first generation of the *Nyugat* circle.

The 1920s were as wild in Hungary as elsewhere; the country's expressions of the Jazz Age are reflected in the work of Gyula Krúdy (1878–1933) as well as in the operettas of Franz Lehár and Emmerich Kalmán. In contrast, László Németh (1901–74) and Gyula Illyés (1902–83) depicted social misery and rural drudgery while the sceptical socialist Tibor Déry (1894–1977) denounced the more absurd aspects of social development.

Modern Hungarian Art

Contemporary Hungarian artists include writers György Konrád, Péter Nádas and Péter Esterházy, the artist Lajos Kassák and the sculptor Imre Varga. Others, who expressed their talents as part of the Hungarian diaspora, include the abstract painter Victor Vasarely, who founded the Op Art movement, and the film director István Szabó, who rose to international fame with films he shot abroad (and who won an Oscar for *Mephisto*). Today Budapest's art scene is an exciting one in which international influences combine with the talents of local artists to produce numerous original cultural treasures.

Left: an abstract work by a modern artist

HISTORY HIGHLIGHTS

1st century BC Celts establish the fortified village of *Ak-Ink* ('ample water') at the hot springs on the western bank of the Danube.

AD198 The Roman provincial town of Aquincum is promoted to the status of a *colonia*; 60,000 civilians and around 10,000 soldiers reside in the area of today's Óbuda.

450 Attila the Hun takes up residence close to the city surrendered by the Romans.

896 The nomadic Magyars occupy the country.

1000 King Stephen (later canonised as St Stephen) introduces Christianity as the state religion. After receiving papal recognition, the Kingdom of Hungary becomes part of Western Christendom.

1061 First written reference to Pest, the settlement on the east bank of the Danube.

1241 After an attack by Mongols, local settlers take refuge on the hill above the west bank. This settlement eventually develops into the royal city of Buda.

1458–90 Hungary and its capital, Buda, flourish under King Mátyás Corvinus.

1526–41 After the battle of Mohács, the Turks conquer what is effectively today's Hungary. Buda becomes a Turkish provincial capital for the next 150 years.

1686 A Christian army recaptures Buda, destroying it in the process. The Habsburgs of Austria don the crown of St Stephen.

1703–11 Hungarian rebellion against foreign rule, led by Ferenc II Rákóczi.

1848–9 The Habsburgs, assisted by Russian troops, crush Lajos Kossuth's Hungarian freedom fighters.

1867 The historic Austro-Hungarian Compromise is signed by the Austrian foreign minister Count von Beust.

1867–1918 Under the terms of the Austro-Hungarian Dual Monarchy, Hungarians are granted autonomy. Budapest, which was united in 1872, becomes an international city.

1918–9 The monarchy is defeated and Hungary becomes a republic. Neither national nor socialist revolutionaries succeed in attempted coups.

1919 Admiral Horthy assumes power after Hungary's humiliating defeat in World War I. Hungary is forced to cede three-fifths of its land to neighbouring states.

1939–45 Allied with the Axis powers, Hungary is again on the losing side in World War II. In 1944 German troops occupy the country; Budapest is severely damaged.

1946–8 Once more a republic, Hungary is ruled for two years by a government of civic reformers.

1949 Communists supported by the Soviet Union take power.

1956 On 23 October, students in Budapest protest against Stalinist terror; large sections of the population and even the army join them. Soviet tanks crush all hopes of freedom. Reformers' leader Imre Nagy is executed.

1956–89 János Kádár runs the country under the motto 'Those who are not against us are with us'. His 'goulash communism' lays the political foundations of the peaceful revolution of 1989.

1990 A conservative administration is voted into power.

1994 A disillusioned electorate returns the reformed socialists to power under the leadership of Gyula Horn.

1998 Viktor Orbán becomes prime minister. In its third free elections, Budapest votes for Gabor Demosky as mayor.

1999 Hungary joins NATO.

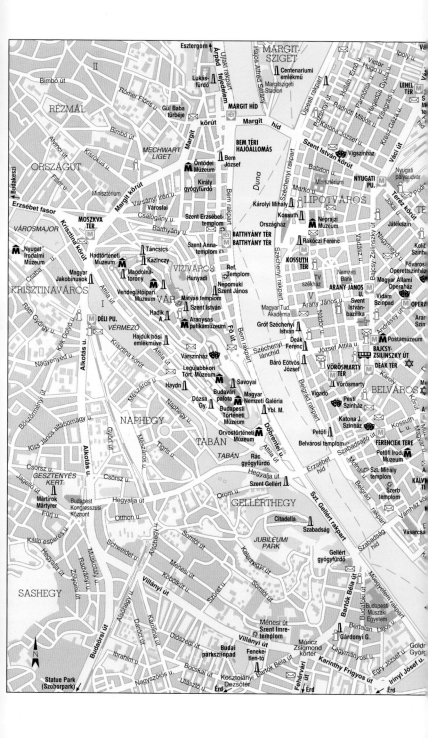

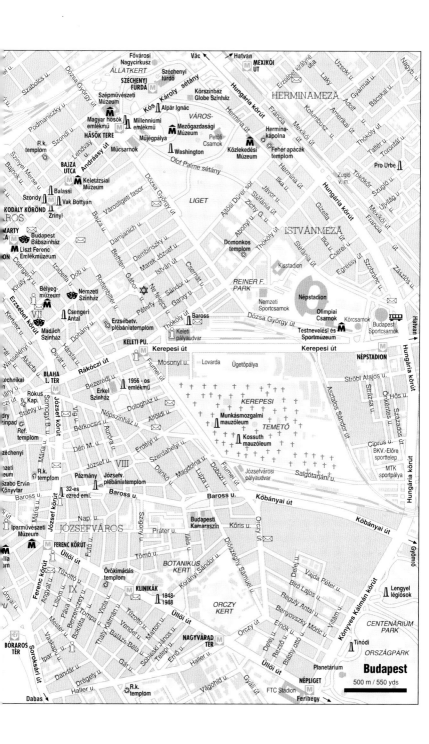

Budapest

500 m / 550 yds

City Itineraries

Budapest, one of the most magnificently situated cities in the world, does not *lie* on the Danube: the river flows *through* it, as if attempting to divide the city. That it does not succeed is thanks to the presence of a number of handsome bridges that maintain the union between Buda and Pest. To the west, on the Buda side, stands Várgehy (Castle Hill), Mátyás church and the Fishermen's Bastion; further to the south is the Gellérthegy with its famous thermal baths. Viziváros (Water City) and Óbuda lie to the north, as do the ruins of the ancient Roman city of Aquincum.

Pest, to the east, where the modern city first developed, is the adminstrative and commercial centre. This is where you will find the majority of the city's shops, restaurants and various nightlife options. This area is dominated by the massive Parliament Building, to the south of which are the Danube Promenade and Váci utca – the main shopping streets in the city centre. Pest's major roads are the semi-circular Nagykörút (Great) boulevard and the Kiskörút (Small) boulevard. Of the main axial streets that radiate from these, the most famous is Andrássy út, a long, tree-shaded avenue leading out to Városliget (City Park), the zoo and the Széchenyi Baths.

Budapest's three Metro lines are sensibly laid out and all intersect at Deák tér in the middle of Pest. Further public transport (in which Budapestik – as the city's natives are known – seem to prefer standing to sitting) is provided by the bus and tram systems. At their termini are connections to the surrounding area via the suburban HÉV railway system. The railway stations are the most confusing thing about Budapest. Most international and domestic trains for the north and the northeast arrive at and depart from the Keleti pályaudvar (East Station), but both it and the Nyugati pályaudvar (East Station) – where trains from the west also arrive – lie on the Pest side, that is, in the eastern part of the city. Déli pályaudvar (South Station), for trains to Lake Balaton, lies over on the west, in Buda, beyond Castle Hill.

Central Europe's Answer To Paris

The Danube, a river whose sheer romance has inspired artists, writers and composers down the centuries, is not the city's only aquatic claim to fame: there are more than 100 thermal springs in Budapest, which enjoys the distinction of being the only capital city in the world that is also a spa resort. On terra firma the city is known as 'the Paris of Central Europe' due to its coffee houses, pavement cafés, a wine-producing hinterland and frequently encountered public scenes of unabashed affection. Budapest's location in the centre of the country makes it a good base from which to explore other parts of Hungary.

Left: laurel wreathed statue on Váci Utca
Right: a city chef

1. CASTLE HILL *(see map below)*

Enjoy a leisurely stroll through the ancient romantic streets of the castle quarter in Buda, where you can visit the castle and its museums, the Mátyás Church and the Fishermen's Bastion – all the while enjoying superb views of the city. All Budapest museums are open daily, 10am–6pm except Monday and the day after a public holiday.

To the start: either walk across the Széchenyi lánchíd (Chain Bridge) to Clark Ádám Square, from where you can board the funicular railway (Sikló) for the short ride to the summit of Castle Hill; or take the Metro (M2) to Moscow Square and there board the No 16 bus which wends its way up Castle Hill to Dísz tér (see below), in the heart of Castle Hill. Note that private motor vehicles are normally banned from Castle Hill.

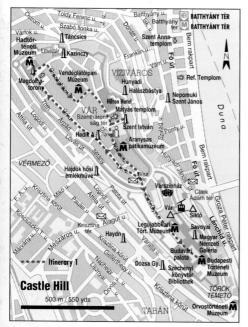

Castle Hill

500 m / 550 yds

From the funicular, turn half-right, leaving the castle to your left, and pass alongside the impressive yellow **Várszínház** building. Originally this was a Carmelite monastery but after the dissolution of the Carmelite order, part of it was turned into a theatre. It was here that the first ever Hungarian-language dramatic production took place in 1790. The building's wooden supports collapsed in 1924 and it was eventually rebuilt in 1978. Today it features regular performances by members of the National Theatre.

A left turn takes you into **Dísz tér**. Exit on the far side of the square on Uri utca, the road to the left of the **Honved Memorial** that

Above: the castle on the hill

commemorates the heroes of the 1948–49 War of Independence. At No 9 you'll come to the entrance to the **Labyrinth**. In Ottoman times, these limestone caverns under the hill were turned into a 10-km (6-mile) system of passages and chambers. They also served as an air-raid shelter during World War II. A handful of enterprising young entrepreneurs now provide guided tours of the caverns and passageways and have lined the route with wax figures taken from Hungarian history. In fact the place is a cross between a geological-historical museum and a ghost train.

Further along the road, immediately beyond an equestrian statue of the bold hussar András Hadik (a former castle commander of Buda and a favourite of Empress Maria Theresa) you will reach Szentháromság utca and, to the right, your first view of Mátyás church. Proceeding towards the church you might stop for coffee at No 7, the **Ruszwurm Coffee House**. Even in Vienna, the home of the coffee-house, Ruszwurm is held in high esteem. Or visit No 6, the **House of Hungarian Wines** (daily 11am–7pm) and sample some of the 500 wines tastefully displayed in beautifully appointed cellars.

Christian Worship

Postpone your visit to the Mátyás church and return to Uri utca, where you can admire the Gothic facade of the house at No 31. At the end of the road stands the rather isolated **Mary Magdalene Tower**, which has degenerated

into a souvenir shop. Its former function becomes clear when you notice the wall foundations of the medieval Franciscan church behind it. This was the only church in the castle quarter that the Turks allowed the local Christian population to use: Catholics were permitted to pray in the choir while Protestants were given the nave.

Beyond the church, **Kapisztrán Square** is flanked on the left by a former barracks, which today houses the **Museum of Military History**. There are splendid views of the Buda hills from the terrace in front of the museum. Exit from the eastern side of Kapisztrán Square and to the left you will notice the enormous neo-Romanesque complex of the **National Archives** with its distinctive multicoloured roof. On the other side of the road is a series of charming houses with late baroque facades and a late 19th-century **Lutheran Church** which sometimes holds concerts in the summer. The **Vienna Gate** to the right of the National Archives conveniently leads from Castle Hill down to Moscow Square Metro station. On the right, just before you reach the square, is the **Aranaykaviár** restaurant (Ostrom utca 19; tel: 201 6737), which is famous for its Russian cuisine.

Above: lending a feminine touch to Országház utca

While on Castle Hill, turn back from Kapisztrán Square and return towards Mátyás church by taking **Országház utca** (Parliament Street), which runs parallel to Uri utca. This street owes its name to the baroque building at No 28, where the Hungarian Parliament debated the burning issues of the day in the early 19th century. Today concerts and events sponsored by the Hungarian Academy of Science are held here. Medieval houses at Nos 18, 20 and 22 give an idea of the neighbourhood's appearance in centuries past.

Turn left at the short second street and, at the left corner on Fortuna utca, you will find the **Museum of Commerce and Catering** (No 4). This museum contains lots of fascinating exhibits on the country's 20th-century cultural and social history. On leaving the museum, go back (southwards) to Becsu kepu ter and then make a U-turn into **Táncsics Mihály utca**. It was in this street

that the Jewish community lived in medieval times. The building at No. 26, one of several synagogues to be uncovered in this street, is now a **Jewish museum** with frescoes, original Hebrew inscriptions and other artefacts. Across the road at No. 7 is the baroque **Erdody Palace**, which is now a **Museum of Musical History**. Beethoven lived here for a short period in 1800. The museum has a fine collection of old musical instruments, including those used by an orchestra in Haydn's time, and an exhibition devoted to Béla Bartók.

A Literary Restaurant

Continue southwards on Fortuna utca towards Mátyás Church and you will immediately enter **Hess András Square**, named after the brilliant Renaissance printer. Despite the square's name, the monument here is not of András but of Pope Innocent XI. Behind the monument is the **Red Hedgehog** architectural complex, parts of which have stood on this site since 1390. On another side of the square is the Hilton Hotel, opposite which a pleasant courtyard features souvenir stores, a restaurant and, for a fine selection of travel and art literature which you can read over coffee and cake, **Litea**.

If your hunger demands a more substantial meal, you should try the upmarket **Pest-Buda** (Fortuna utca 3; tel: 356 9849 – bookings advisable). An alternative is the **Alabárdos** (Országház utca 2, tel: 356 0851 – bookings advisable), where gothic arcades, lute music and candle-lit tables exude a medieval atmosphere. Less heavy on the senses, and pocket, is the **Fekete Holló** (Országház utca 10; tel: 356 0175). All three restaurants are particularly good at dusk when, illumined by glowing streetlamps, the castle quarter is at its most romantic. The restaurants at the **Hilton Hotel** (Hess András tér; tel: 214 3000) are also recommended.

The Hilton opened in 1976 and is definitely worth a visit – seldom have medieval and modern styles been blended so harmoniously in a single

Above: Mátyás church reflected in the windows of the Hilton Hotel

city itineraries

building. The objective during construction was to maintain the character of the surrounding buildings: the cloister of the Dominican monastery was cleverly converted into a foyer that often hosts concerts. The remains of a Gothic tower and the walls that once surrounded the choir of the church of St Nicholas give the hotel facade its distinctive appearance. Reflections of the surrounding buildings in the hotel's windows make fascinating details.

Next door, the **Mátyás (Matthias) Church** attracts large crowds, not least as a result of its proximity to the Hilton. The church's early-Gothic foundation walls were subjected to extravagant decoration 100 years ago but today the most attractive aspect of the facade is its reflection in the hotel.

Even the interior fails to exude any sense of Gothic space. The wall paintings are somewhat far-fetched and light enters through garish modern windows, but the church nevertheless enthralls locals and tourists alike. As old as Buda itself, it was used as a parish church by the local German population in the 13th century.

The church was given its current name in the 15th century, when King Mátyás Corvinus was married here, twice. The church underwent a baroque conversion, after which it was restored in neo-Gothic style towards the end of the 19th century. Fortunately the architect, Frigyes Schulek, took care to keep the few original fragments that remained. The 80-m (262-ft) tower, and

Above: Mátyás church entices locals and visitors
Right: the kitsch Fishermen's Bastion

the northern chapels with their colourful roof tiles constitute the kind of architectural mix that typifies Budapest. Take a pinch of everything: a spoonful of Gothic, a touch of Art Nouveau, a drop of neoclassicism and a lot of imagination; stir, add some colourful icing and you have the Budapest Romantic style. Also created according to this recipe, the **Fishermen's Bastion** next to the church is an amazing piece of kitsch. After Schulek had finished his work on Mátyás church he gave full rein to his architectural fantasies on the section of the hill once defended by the Fishermen's Guild. The result has been copied by Disneyland.

Early in the 20th century, when the construction work on the Bastion was completed, the mighty bronze equestrian **statue of St Stephen** was unveiled in the square (**Trinity Square**). Incidentally, the famous crown of St Stephen, Hungary's first Christian monarch, is on display in the National Museum; the crown in the Mátyás Church Museum is a replica. In the centre of the square, in front of the church and at the highest point of Castle Hill, stands the **Trinity Column**. This baroque masterpiece was created in 1713 following an outbreak of the plague that resulted in numerous deaths.

The three rooms of the **Pharmaceutical Museum** (Tárnok utca No 18), a few steps further in the direction of the castle, are fascinating. Probably the most interesting exhibit is the alchemist's workshop, which is full of mysterious paraphernalia and magical substances. The friendly museum attendants, all of whom are female, are much taken by the fact that the late prime minister Jozsef Antall wrote a learned brochure on the museum.

Helen's Heartbreak

Continue on Tárnok utca to return to Dísz tér, where the **Corona Coffee House** is a good bet for afternoon refreshment. Then retrace your morning steps and, on passing the funicular, immediately enter the **castle-palace complex**. The buildings here, restored after World War II, no longer house any official departments but are used purely for museums. You should allow at least two hours for a visit to the castle buildings. En route to the museums, observe on the rear wall of St George's Square (the Outer Courtyard) the **King Mátyás Fountain**, whose bronze figures relate a tragic legend: Helen was a beautiful peasant girl who met the king while he was hunting incognito. She fell in love with him, but when she discovered his true identity and thus realised the futility of her desire, she died of a broken heart. Somewhat incongruously, the centre of the courtyard features a statue of a cowboy in full regalia breaking in a headstrong horse.

The **Ludwig Museum**, which can be reached from the Outer Courtyard, features a collection of the works of 1960s and '70s pop artists such as Roy Lichtenstein, Robert Rauschenberg and Claes Oldenburg. The museum also has a pleasant, uncrowded café with views of the Buda Hills. Adjoining the museum is the **Hungarian National Gallery** – enter from the Danube side of the palace. The **statue of Prince**

Left: St Stephen. **Above Right:** in the castle's courtyard. **Right:** Castle Hill at dusk

Eugene of Savoy (who successfully fought the Turks) outside the entrance is considered to be the best equestrian statue in Budapest. The gallery occupies the three main wings of the castle and it is the perfect place for obtaining an overview of Hungarian painting and sculpture from the Middle Ages until well into the 20th century. The Gothic masterpieces hanging on the first floor and the Impressionist paintings on the second storey are especially noteworthy.

The Budapest Manuscripts

Situated behind the National Gallery and overlooking the Buda Hills, the **National Library** contains about six million books, more than 625,000 manuscripts and nearly 200,000 maps. Yet for all the collection's immensity, the undoubted highlight is the 'Budapest Manuscripts', which are some of the oldest known medieval scripts. To the south of the National Gallery is the **History** or **Castle Museum**. Here you will find diverse sculptures, weapons and artefacts, all representing a stage in the city's 2,000-year history. Moreover, the museum exhibits the excavated remains and reconstructed fortifications of the medieval royal palace.

From the front of the castle you can take the funicular – or, if you have the energy, descend by steps and paved paths – to the level of the Danube and Clark Ádám Square. Alternatively, head for Moscow Square through the Vienna Gate. Another option, applicable during library hours, is to take the lift to **Dózsa György tér**, at the rear of Castle Hill, where there is a tram stop.

city itineraries

2. DOWNTOWN IN PEST *(see map, p30)*

Wend your way through the centre of Pest – taking in Vörösmarty tér, Váci utca and the Inner Ring Road – and see the National Museum's splendid collection. Enjoy lunch and dinner at the Hotel Astoria.

To the start: metro M1 to Vörösmarty tér or M2 or M3 to Deák tér from which a 300-metre/yard walk along Deák Ferenc utca leads to Vörösmarty tér.

The city centre underwent a tremendous amount of rebuilding following the Austro-Hungarian Compromise of 1867 but no further urban centres arose in the suburbs beyond the Outer Ring. The heart of Pest thus remains the Belváros (Inner City) and Vörösmarty tér remains the main hub of social activities. All three Metro lines intersect at nearby Deák tér.

Not all of the buildings on **Vörös-marty tér** are reminders of the glorious past: the functional and modern **House of Music** has a concert hall, the largest music shop in the city and an art gallery. The Art Nouveau buildings opposite are altogether more pleasing to the eye. The **Luxus department store** within these buildings was, until the economic and political liberalisation of the early 1980s, the best shop in the city for quality and variety. Today it is privately run and still considered a good address.

On the north side of the square, the venerable **Café Gerbeaud** is the ultimate nostalgic Budapest coffee house. Founded in 1870 and taken over by Swiss confectioner Emile Gerbaud in 1884, the café is famous for its home-made specialities and the superb atmosphere of its three elegant rooms. If you're here in the summer, take advantage of the outdoor terrace.

Top: Mihály Vörösmarty recites his *Ode to the Fatherland* in Vörösmarty tér
Above: Café Gerbeaud is famous for its home-made specialities

In the centre of the square a monument to the poet and patriot **Mihály Vörösmarty** (1800–55) is surrounded by several stone 'groupies' who listen as he declaims his *Ode to the Fatherland*. The first verse, beginning with the words, 'Love and loyalty to the fatherland in you, O Hungarian, ever shall remain!', is hewn into the statue's plinth. To protect the statue's Carrara marble, the monument is wrapped in plastic sheeting in winter. In spring, the wrapping is removed and the square becomes a charming marketplace filled with portrait-painters, street peddlers and performing youngsters.

Colourful Characters

There's something happening throughout the year in the nearby **Váci utca** pedestrian precinct, which emerges from the south side of the square. Activity during the day focuses on the numerous exclusive shops; in the evening on the bars, restaurants, nightclubs and gambling dens that now thrive in and around the Váci utca. The precinct's numerous colourful characters include ethnic Hungarians from Romanian Transylvania who try to keep body and soul together by selling hand-woven materials, embroidered cloths, furs and leather goods. A stroll along Váci utca not only acquaints you with the bustle of a 21st-century capital city: it also offers several glimpses into its history. At the first side-street that you reach there is evidence of the medieval town wall that marked the municipal border of Pest until 1789. It was then that the area around the tower known as the *Váco kup* became so crowded by the growing population that the tower and the walls had to be pulled down. A marker on the plaster recalls the original city limits.

Take time to examine No 9 on Váci utca: this building, which still has a striking Art Nouveau interior, is the home of the Pest Theatre, which stages classical drama. The theatre was once occupied by the Inn of Seven Electors, and the 12-year-old prodigy Franz Liszt performed here. At No 11, the Thonet House is recognisable by its facade of decorative Zsolnay tiles. Also check out the **Hermes Fountain** with its elegant statue. Postmodern architecture made a late start in Budapest in the shape of the **Hotel Taverna**, built in 1985. Across the street the **Millennium Centre** is a small mall occupied mainly by upmarket clothes stores.

Back on the left of the street turn into **Haris köz**. Towards the end of the 19th century a speculator opened this alley (*köz* means 'narrow passageway') to the public as a means of increasing the value of his property. (To keep his ownership rights, he had to close the passageway for at least one day each year.) From the right side of Haris köz you can enter the ornate and cavernous **Párizsi Udvar** (Paris shopping arcade), with its stained-glass cupola. To fully

Above: riding the lion

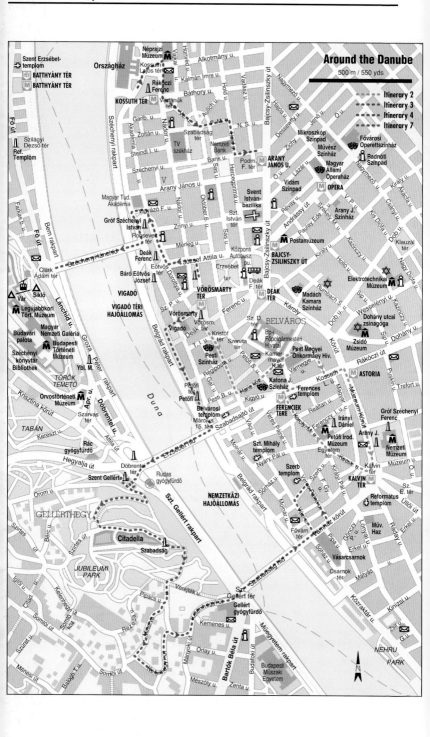

appreciate the beauty of this arcade you should enter from Kígyó utca, which runs parallel to Haris köz. Also in this building, the **IBUSZ** main office offers a range of tourist services.

Back on Haris köz, cross Petőfi Sándor utca, and Haris köz becomes Pilvax köz. Note, on the right, the **Café Pilvax**, the newest edition of a famous old café where revolutionaries gathered to decide on their radical programme for national independence in March 1848.

You now emerge into another square, Kamermayer Károly. Turn left here and enter Városház utca, which is dominated by the massive **Town Hall**. This building started out in 1711 as a hospital for 4,000 soldiers wounded in the Turkish wars. Later it became the Austrian grenadiers' Charles Barracks before metamorphosing into the city's main administration building in 1894. It is the largest baroque building in Budapest, and Queen Maria Theresa claimed that it was more beautiful than the town hall in Vienna. Above the side entrance next to the main door reliefs illustrate the military exploits of Charles III and Prince Eugene of Savoy. Unfortunately Városház utca is now so narrow that the original impression of size and space has been lost.

Secessionist Mosaic

A few steps further leads, on the left, to **Martinelli tér**. On the left of this square is the baroque 18th-century **Servite church** and, facing you, the **Turkish Bank**, which has a glorious Secessionist mosaic that dates back to 1906. Entitled *Glory To Hungary*, the mosaic depicts Hungarian pilgrims – a category that includes political heroes such as István Széchenyi and Lajos Kossuth – paying homage to the Virgin Mary.

Backtrack now to Kamermayer Károly tér, on the far side of which is the massive **Komitat House (Pest County Hall)**, the administrative centre for the country's 14 regions and five major cities. Virtually all of Hungary is run from here: regional self-government remains practically nonexistent, even after the 1989 revolution. Beyond its distinctive facade on Városház utca, the Komitat House has three magnificent inner courtyards that host classical concerts during the summer months – usually on Monday evenings.

Exit the square by Vitkovics Mihály utca, where picturesque shops sell wares such as hats, furs, gloves and jewellery. **The Galerie Bar**, with its discreet atmosphere, is a good place to enjoy a preprandial refreshment.

Above: the Arany statue at the entrance to the National Museum
Right: one of many ancient treasures and artefacts exhibited by the museum

Turn right into **Semmelweis utca**, one of the few inner-city avenues to have benefited from preservation orders, and follow it for a couple of hundred metres. Turn left into **Kossuth Lajos utca** and very soon you will reach the **Inner Ring Road**, with Károly körút to the left and Múzeum körút to the right.

Diagonally opposite, the impressive glass-covered building is one of the most up-to-date business centres in Budapest. Investors come here to buy anything from luxury cars to ready-made factories. The Hungarian government and Western entrepreneurs obviously want to turn Budapest into the centre of trade and investment within the former Eastern bloc. State-of-the-art office blocks and department stores like this are springing up like mushrooms all over the city.

Gypsy Orchestra

The **Hotel Astoria**, on the other corner of Kossuth Lajos utca and Múzeum körút, is a good choice for a leisurely lunch. Although its three stars are somewhat faded these days, its café and restaurant have retained their late 19th-century atmosphere. Everything is wonderfully old-fashioned, and a *primas* performs with his gypsy orchestra in the evening. It's worth having an evening meal here just for the experience. A good alternative for dinner (and lunch) is the more traditional, inexpensive **Csendes** (Múzeum körút, entrance at Ferenczi István utca 3; tel: 267 0218;noon–10pm except Sun).

After lunch stroll along Múzeum körút and, on the left, after several hundred metres, you will find yourself in front of the neoclassical portico of the **National Museum**, which is famous for its historical exhibits, notably the royal crown and insignia of Hungary. Across the road, two good antiques shops are worth checking out: the **Központi Antikvárium** at No 15, and the **Honterus Antikvárium** at No 35. Some of the gaps between these *antikvária* reveal impressive glimpses of sections of the medieval town wall. Múzeum körút leads into busy Kálvin tér with its elegant **Reformed Church**.

On the right of the square, walk beneath the Bridge of Sighs, which

Above: University Church ceiling
Right: the Franciscan Church

connects two buildings belonging to the **Hotel Korona**, to enter Kecskeméti utca. This street is lined with well-preserved houses dating from the period of rapid industrial expansion in the latter years of the 19th century. It leads on the left to the **University Church**, whose two mighty towers form an obvious landmark. Unfortunately its baroque splendour has been somewhat marred by the rise of the surrounding hotel buildings. Continue along Kecskeméti utca as it becomes Károlyi Mihály utca. On the right, you pass the classical **Károlyi Palace**, now a museum that has memorabilia pertaining to – and texts by – Sándor Petőfi (1823–49), Hungary's national poet.

Café for the Literati

At the corner with Reáltanoda utca, a domed tower with the now familiar Zsolnay tiles dominates. The tower is part of the **University Library**. Check out its coffee shop, where you sit under the watchful eyes of Homer and Herodotus, Cicero and Plato, and among the work of the 19th-century fresco painter Károly Lotz. The first-floor reading room, where there are more fine Lotz frescoes, is also open to the public. Alternatively you could cross the road to the **Centrál Café**. This was once a renowned literary hang-out, and now it lives again in all its old elegance. Whether you order a full meal or just a coffee, you will probably appreciate the 19th-century decor.

You will soon reach Kossuth Lajos, where, at the corner, you will find the somewhat inconspicuous **Franciscan Church** built in Italian baroque style. The church door is adorned with the Franciscan symbol that depicts St Francis of Assisi and the bleeding hands of Christ. On the left wall as you enter the church is a large plaque commemorating the devastation wreaked by the floods of 1838 that resulted in the deaths of more than 400 people. A small arrow indicates the heights reached by the Danube on that tragic occasion. Inside the church you can see magnificent baroque altars and more frescoes by Lotz. If you turn right along Kossuth Lajos, you should arrive back at the Astoria just in time for dinner.

Above: the University Library

3. ALONG THE DANUBE *(see map, p30)*

Stroll along the Danube Promenade and cross the Elisabeth Bridge to the massive limestone cliff of Gellérthegy and the Gellért Baths.

To the start: take Metro M3 and alight at Vörösmarty tér.

The **Danube Promenade** (Duna-korzó), running between the Chain Bridge and the Elisabeth Bridge on the Pest side of the river, was once Budapest's biggest attraction. In the late 19th and early 20th centuries elegant hotels such as the Carlton and the Ritz lined the Danube here, as did many gourmet restaurants and coffee houses. Cosmopolitan society used to congregate at these cafés, and many fashionable figures could be observed as they took their constitutionals along the banks of the Danube. They were joined by

members of the upper classes, locals from the suburbs, penniless bohemians, adventurers and ladies of ill repute. This peaceful, sophisticated scene was shattered for ever by World War II. When the destruction was over, the populace had neither the ambition nor the imagination to rebuild what had been lost. Since then the people of Budapest have had to content themselves with a pale shadow of the promenade's former glory.

Promenade to the Concert Hall

To reach the Danube Promenade from Vörösmarty tér, stroll westwards for a couple of hundred metres on Deák Ferenc utca, passing through an open square, Vigadó tér. At the promenade you will find pleasure-cruise boats and stalls selling

Above: view from the top of the Gellérthegy
Left: the Inner City Main Parish Church

embroidery, leather goods and souvenirs. The rear of the square is dominated by the majestic **Vigadó** concert hall, which originally opened in 1865. Imaginatively and colourfully decorated by the architect Frigyes Feszl, it is another fine example of Budapest's synthesis of styles.

The Hungarian word *vigadó* conjures up images of happiness and enjoyment but the hall's history has hardly lived up to its name. Music lovers waited patiently from the end of the war until 1980 for it to reopen, and many were then unimpressed by the first concert. The audience was enthralled by the magnificent setting that had been so painstakingly restored, but the musicians complained about the poor quality of the acoustics in the nearly 20-metre (65-ft) high hall – just as their forebears had done 100 years earlier. The people of Budapest nevertheless adore the Vigadó: its 800 seats are sold out for every concert and today it has a restaurant to the left of the back stalls. New Year's Eve *Live From the Vigadó* shows, featuring excerpts from Hungarian operettas, have been broadcast across Europe. The modern-art gallery in the right wing of the building also has a great claim on the affections of the nation. Any artist whose work is displayed here is bound to provoke a countrywide reaction.

From Vigadó ter, walk upstream along the Korsó, which is separated from the river by tracks for the No 2 tram – and pass the Inter-Continental and Atrium Hyatt hotels. These ugly concrete blocks rise above the Danube with no sense of line or proportion, and no attempt was made to integrate them into their surroundings. Even the hotels' stylish interiors cannot compensate for the aberrations of 1980s architecture. As you head downstream past Vigadó tér, things get worse: the **Hotel Duna-Marriott** represents the soulless architecture of the 1960s: the building is nothing more than a suburban block of flats dolled up to look like a luxury hotel. Give its terrace a miss, despite its fine view – a continuation of your stroll along the riverbank will yield sights of far greater interest.

1956 Uprising

Next is a small park containing a statue of the national poet Sándor Petőfi. It was his recital of his poem *Talpra Magyar* ('Rise, Hungarian') on the steps of the National Museum that sparked the 1848 revolution. It also gave the Hungarians' struggle against Austria a lyrical leitmotif. More than 100 years later, on 23 October 1956, hundreds of students gathered at the statue to demonstrate against the Soviet Union and its obedient puppet, Matyas Rákosi. Then, once again, Petőfi's patriotic poem was of burning relevance. During the ensuing procession past the Hungarian Radio building, Soviet troops fired on the peaceful demonstrators, resulting in the first fatalities of a revolution that was brutally crushed.

At the back of this park stands the **Greek Orthodox Church**, which was constructed between 1791 and 1794 with money donated by Greek merchants. Visitors are welcome – don't miss the magnificent iconostasis. Services are held in Hungarian but correspond to Greek ritual.

The **Belvárosi Plébániatemplom** (Inner City Main Parish

Right: monument to Sándor Petőfi

Church) is the city's most interesting church. Its plain baroque facade is almost hidden by the six-lane ramp of the Elisabeth Bridge, but its twin towers face the Danube. It began life in the 13th century as a three-aisled Romanesque cathedral, and somehow its long choir, ribbed vault and some of its windows survived Hitler's bombs. The Turks turned it into a mosque, and you can see the niche (*mihrab*) indicating the direction of Mecca, towards which they prayed.

Excavations in front of the church have revealed the foundations of a **Roman military camp** at the spot where, at 285 metres (930ft), the Danube reaches its narrowest point. To get to the Buda side of the river cross **Elisabeth Bridge** (Erzsébet híd), which was opened to traffic in 1964, almost 20 years after retreating German troops blew up the bridges across the Danube. All that could be safely salvaged from the original Elisabeth Bridge (completed towards the end of the 19th century) were its piers.

An Unfortunate Bishop

Turn left and walk south for about 1,000 metres (3,300ft) between the river and the **Gellérthegy**, a massive, tree-covered limestone cliff named after Bishop Gellért (Gerhard) of Csanád. The unfortunate prelate was tied to a cart and pushed off the edge of the cliff by Magyar heathens, who had no intention of complying with their king's invitation to join the Christian faith. On the site of the murder there stands a larger-than-life bronze statue of St Gellért astride an artificial waterfall. To reach the Citadel and the Freedom Statue, from which there are superb views of the city, cross the road at the next bridge and take any of the footpaths that wend their way around the hill. Allow about 40 minutes to get there by foot. Alternatively board a No 27 bus at Móricz Zsigmond körtér.

The **Citadel** was built by the Austrians as a military bastion from which they could keep an eye on the city and the hill after

Above: the Gellért Baths' thermal swimming pool
Left: classical motifs adorn Gellért Baths' interiors

the Hungarian revolutionaries were defeated in 1848-9. This fortress is now a tourist attraction, complete with restaurant and café. You could stop here for lunch; otherwise wait for about 30 minutes until you reach the Hotel Gellért's pleasant coffee house and fine restaurant (tel: 385 2200).

The **Liberation Memorial** on the viewing terrace, erected in 1947, depicts a woman holding a palm branch over her head. It is said that the monument was commissioned by Admiral Horthy in memory of his son István, who was killed in a plane crash. The palm branch replaced the original propellor. At the same time a statue of a Red Army soldier was placed at the base to commemorate those Soviet soldiers who died liberating Budapest from the Nazis. After the events of 1990, this reminder of the Red Army's power, albeit in the historic context of liberating Hungary, was bound to be unpopular, and some of the more allegorical works surrounding The Lady were removed.

High Living

The 20-minute descent from the cliff passes through a former vineyard en route to the **Hotel Gellért**, via several stone stairways and paths. Make a minor detour in the park if you want to see a few of the fine villas along the **Minerva utca**, especially the studio house at Kelenhegyi út 12–14. The **Gellért Thermal Baths** complex (generally Mon–Fri 6am–7pm, Fri, Sat 6am–5pm; tel: 466 6166) next to the hotel (enter from Kelenhegyi út) has swimming and thermal pools, a steam room, sauna and massage facilities. There was a hospital on the site in the 13th century, and the Turks had a spa here. Today's spa has a marble-columned indoor swimming pool, a series of thermal pools, a glorious outdoor swimming pool with a wave machine and an area for nude sunbathing. In high summer visitors can swim to musical accompaniment in the outdoor pool (Fri, Sat 8pm–midnight). Such high living is reminiscent of the 1930s and 1940s, when debutantes danced on the glass floor over the pool at the Gellért's balls.

Return to the Pest side of the river via the **Freedom Bridge** (Szabadság híd), built in 1896. This is the finest of the three bridges in the city-centre area, and reflects the exuberance and variety that characterises turn-of-the-20th-century Hungarian architecture. On the other side of the river the promenade is dominated by a neo-Renaissance building that served as the harbour customs house and now houses the University of Industrial Science.

Immediately beyond is the spacious **Central Market Hall**, which began to thrive as a modern market in the early 20th century, when supplies were delivered via the Danube and an underground canal. The shopping area, with its galleries and annexes, covers a length of 150 metres/yds. The ground floor features every type of Hungarian produce as well as imported exotic fruits. On the upper floor there is a good selection of embroidered textiles and handicrafts.

Right: the *fin-de-siècle* Freedom Bridge

Opposite the Market Hall is the upper section of **Váci utca** – formerly the southern poor relation of the affluent northern end of the street. In recent years this part of Váci utca has become an elegant shopping thoroughfare. This quarter was in the heart of medieval Pest, as you can see from the remains of the town wall in the parallel street, **Veres Pálné utca**.

In **Szerb utca**, which joins the two streets, the lovely 18th-century **Serbian Orthodox Church** stands in a small garden. Return to Váci utca for a relaxed stroll down the street and enjoy a taste of old and new Budapest. There are still a few junk shops, and some genuine Hungarian pubs hidden behind the fine houses with their run-down facades. A variety of new outlets – antiques shops, art galleries, restaurants – have opened here. Check out the simple Japanese teahouse at No 65, opposite which is the splendidly ornate neo-Renaissance old Budapest city hall. The stylish **Nautilus Restaurant** at No 72 (daily noon–2am; tel: 338 4830) is a good dinner choice. The menu – in English and German – features all kinds of seafood in imaginative variations, and delicious meat dishes such as breast of turkey in roquefort sauce.

4. PARLIAMENT AND ENVIRONS *(see map, p30)*

A short half-day trip taking in the sights around the centre of Pest.

To the start: take Metro line 2 and alight at Kossuth Lajos tér.

Start this tour at the metro exit at the south side of **Kossuth Lajos tér** (named after the leader of the 1848 revolution, whose statue stands in the northern part of the square). The square also features an equestrian monument to **Prince Ferenc II Rákóczi**, another hero in the fight against Habsburg rule.

To the west of the square stands the **Parliament Building**. Construction began in 1885, and although the first session was held in 1896 – 1,000 years after the Magyars occupied the country – the building was completed in 1902. Designed in neo-Gothic style and clearly influenced by London's Houses of Parliament (which seem humble in comparison), this huge edifice stretches 268 metres/yds along the bank of the Danube, its 96-metre (320-ft) high dome towering above it. The impressive limestone facade facing the river, topped by 88 statues of kings, princes and hereditary leaders radiates grandeur. (Conducted tours in English commence at 10am and 2pm. Tickets from 8am at Gate X.)

The main entrance, decorated with lion statues, leads to the ceremonial stairway where Lotz's ceiling frescoes can be seen. On the landing is the bust of the building's designer, Imre Steindl. The staircase leads to the 27-metre (90-ft) high, 16-sided hall, whose pillars are adorned with statues of various Hungarian rulers.

The **Ethnographic Museum** is on the other side of the square, facing the Parliament. This building was constructed at the same time as the Parliament and was formerly the headquarters of the royal law offices and the supreme court of justice. The frescoed ceiling of the monumental central hall shows the figure of Justice with her virtuous and not-so-virtuous sisters. Alternating exhibitions of cultural history and the permanent display of Magyar folk art are both highly informative. The

Left: *Young Peasant With Scythe* statue on Kossuth Lajos tér
Top Right: a lion guards the legislature. **Right:** the Parliament building

tour through the exhibition rooms, which are laid out on a thematic basis, begins on the first floor. Many of the attendants speak English and they do try to answer visitors' questions.

Heroes of 1956

Stroll back towards the south side of Kossuth Lajos tér, where you can get a good cheap snack at **Pick Exklusiv** delicatessen. Then make for a short street, **Vécsey utca**, at the southeast corner of the square, which runs diagonally into Szabadság tér. At the start of the street is a bronze, whimsical, life-size statue of a man on a bridge looking towards parliament. This is Imre Varga's *Witness In Blood*, and the subject is **Imre Nagy**, who was executed after he led the failed uprising of 1956. At the end of the street, in **Szabadság tér** (Liberty Square), is the **Soviet Army Memorial**, an obelisk topped by a Soviet star that honours those Soviet soldiers who fell in Budapest in 1944–45.

To the left as you enter the square is the wedding-cake Európa Bank building and to the right is Hungarian television's headquarters. This massive pile, built in 1905, housed the Stock Exchange until the communists closed it down in 1948. On the left (east side) of the square, at No.12 on the corner of **Perczel Mór utca** and **Sas utca**, is the **US Embassy**. Note the pretty Art Nouveau (or, as it was called in the Austro-Hungarian Empire, Seccessionist) falderals on its facade. Cardinal Mindszenty sheltered here for 15 years after the 1956 uprising.

Perczel Mór utca runs into **Hold utca**. Directly in front of you is the restored **Inner City Market Hall** (Belvárosi Vásárcsarnok), best visited in the morning. Leaving the hall, turn left. On the opposite side of the road is the

delightful, newly restored former **Post Office Savings Bank**. Here, Ödön Lechner combined the curvilinear motifs of Secessionism with motifs from Hungarian folk art to produce, with majolica tiles from Pécs, a light-hearted masterpiece. A bridge joins it with the overbearing **Hungarian National Bank**, built in 1905 from the plans of Ignác Alpár, the architect of the Stock Exchange. The bas-reliefs on the walls – African rug merchants, Magyars ploughing and herding, Vikings loading their longship with loot – are a tribute to commerce. Turn left on **Bank utca** to reach the **Arany János utca** Metro (M3) station.

5. THE DANUBE AND KIRÁLY BATHS *(see map, p41*

Stroll along Buda's Danube Promenade at the foot of Castle Hill, visit Turkish Baths and the Mosque-Tomb of Gül Baba, all in Víziváros.

To the start take Metro M2 and alight at Batthyány tér.

'There is no other town of the land of the faithful, and perhaps in the world, which gushes forth in such wonderful abundance its springs to cure all ills, as Buda.' – Evlllia Chelebi, Middle Age travel writer and historian.

Batthyány tér is overshadowed by the twin towers of the **Church of St Anne**. The church's portal ledge is decorated with allegorical figures representing Faith, Hope and Charity; the middle of the facade features the sculpted figures of St Anne and the Virgin as a child; and the civic arms of Buda and a symbol of the Trinity can be seen in the tympanum. The interior is restrained baroque with a magnificent central high altar surrounded by pillars. It is possible to hear the music of a splendid organ in the loft, but you will have to time your visit carefully. The ground floor of the presbytery houses the spacious yet cosy **Café Angelika** which sometimes hosts poetry readings and other minor cultural events.

There was a time when this café, with its large, imaginative terrace, was an exceptionally popular rendezvous for lovers, and also supposedly for spies – several espionage scandals are said to have resulted from this po-

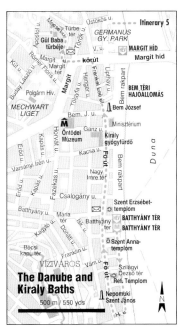

tentially explosive mixture. Spies are presumably thinner on the ground in Budapest these days, but the Café Angelika is still popular with young lovers who have just completed a stroll along the Danube Promenade.

Arrow Cross Massacre

From the church stroll southwards on **Bem rakpart** (Bem quay) alongside the river, following the chestnut trees until you arrive at the neo-Gothic **Reformed Church**. With its slim tower and a roof covered with colourful ceramic tiles, the church is a prominent feature of the Buda skyline. As a result of its fine acoustics, the church's simple interior is often used as a venue for concerts and choral music, so take a look at the noticeboard to see what's on. It was in the lee of this lovely church that the Arrow Cross (Hungarian Nazis) forced thousands of Jews to congregate in the winter of 1944/5 prior to their massacre. The victims were bound together and tossed into the freezing river.

One block further on, turn right into **Halasz utca** where the inexpensive **Dunaparti** is a good place for morning coffee. At the end of Halasz utca turn right into **Fő utca**, which immediately widens out into **Corvin tér**, a somewhat unattractive square which has some baroque houses and a fountain adorned with a statue of a Hungarian warrior. The northern side of the square is dominated by the Buda **Redoubt** – Buda's answer to Pest's Vigadó concert hall. From the square there is a view of Castle Hill, Fishermen's Bastion and Mátyás Church.

Backtrack to Batthyány tér on Fő utca and about 1km (½ mile) after the square you will see, on the left, the **Király Turkish Baths** (Nos 82–86). This is one of the city's finest monuments of the Ottoman period. If you do not wish to try the baths, the route continues northwards along Frankel Leó út. On reaching Margaret Bridge, turn left onto **Margit utca** and, after about 150 metres-yds, turn right at **Mecset utca**. About 80 metres (260ft) on, several flights of stairs lead to the tomb of **Gül Baba** (Tues–Sun 10am–5pm).

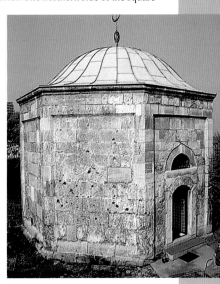

Left: a pleasure cruise about to pass the twin towers of the Church of St Anne
Above: Gül Baba's tomb

Father of the Rose

A Bektashi dervish who distinguished himself during the Sultan's military campaigns, Gül Baba is known as the Father of the Rose. According to the legend, it was he who introduced the cultivation of roses to Buda, although this is unlikely. After his death in 1541, just days after the Turks took Buda, his tomb became a destination for Muslim pilgrims. The site consists of a small octagonal building standing on a colonnaded platform on which there is a small rose garden. In the tomb, the sarcophagus of Gül Baba is covered with a green shroud on which are quotations from the Koran. Many Muslim pilgrims still make the journey to this pleasant, peaceful spot, where there is a fine café complete with views of the city.

Baths

Listed below are some of the baths in Budapest whose thermal springs might appeal to the visitor. The Gellert (indoor and outdoor), the Lukacs (outdoor), the Rudas (indoor) and the Szécheny (outdoor) all have swimming pools. Note that the opening times listed apply to the thermal baths; opening times for the swimming pools might differ slightly.

Gellért Thermal Baths: Kelenhegyi út 4–6, tel: 466 6166.
Men & Women (separate sections), Mon–Fri 6am–7pm, Sat, Sun 6am–5pm.
Sybaritic pleasures in an Art Nouveau palace. The mud baths close slightly earlier than the times listed above. Probably the most popular of the modern baths on the Danube's right bank.

Király Turkish Baths: Fo u. 82–84, tel: 201 4392.
Men: Mon, Wed, Fri 9am–9pm; Women: Tues, Thurs 6.30am–7pm, Sat 6.30am–1pm.
An authentic Turkish baths dating from the days of the Ottoman Empire, and considered to be the most beautiful of its type, with a glorious skylit dome. Be gay or be warned.

Lukács Baths: Frankel Leó 25–29, tel: 326 1695.
Men & Women, Mon–Sat 6am–7pm, Sun 6am–5pm.
A sprawling 19th-century establishment. The therapeutic parts of the baths can be used only on medical advice but the three thermal swimming pools are open throughout the year. A pleasant courtyard displays inscriptions sent by guests grateful for their restored health. Mud and weight baths are segregated as follows. Men: Tues, Thurs, Sat; Women: Mon, Wed, Fri

Rác Baths: Hadnagy u. 8–10, tel: 356 1010.
Men: Tues, Thurs, Sat; Women: Mon, Wed, Fri, Mon–Sat 6.30am–7pm.
A beautiful cupola from Ottoman times covers the central pool. Often a gay venue.

Rudas Baths: Dobrentei tér 9, tel: 375 8373.
Men only. Mon–Fri 6am–8pm; Sat, Sun 6am–1pm.
Situated at the western bridgehead of Elisabeth Bridge, the Rudas is the most imposing of the Turkish-era baths, with a grand cupola supported by eight columns. The indoor swimming pool, which is open to women as well as men, also serves as a medicinal pool by virtue of its constant 29˚C (84°F) temperature. Often known as 'the baths with the green pillars'.

Széchenyi Thermal Baths: állatkerti krt. 11, tel: 321 0310.
Men & Women Mixed: Mon–Sat 6am–7pm. Separate: Mon–Fri 6am–7pm, Sat 6am–1pm.
Located in Pest's City Park, this is one of the largest spa complexes with outdoor thermal pools in Europe, and has recently been renovated. Three large open-air swimming pools are open throughout the year.

Thermal Baths: Thermal Hotel Margitsziget, tel: 329 2300.
Men & Women: daily 7am–8pm.
A modern, immaculate up-market establishment on Margaret Island that attracts those devoted to health rather than hedonism. The place for state-of-the-art hydrotherapy and physiotherapy. Next to the Grand Hotel, which also has baths, and whose guests can use Thermal Bath facilities.

6. ÓBUDA AND AQUINCUM (see map, p44)

Obuda, the city's oldest neighbourhood, prides itself on having its own identity. The Romans established the town of Aquincum here.

To the start: HÉV from Batthyány tér (via the M2) towards Szentendre; alight at Árpád hid. Make lunch reservations at Sipos Halászkert (tel: 250 1064).

To the right, on leaving the station, an 18th-century palazzo (Szentltélek tér 1) is home of the **Vasarely Museum** (Tues–Sun 10am–6pm, 5pm in winter; tel: 250 1540). Here you will find an extensive collection of works by the abstract painter Victor Vasarely, founder of the Op Art movement that featured vivid colours, geometrical forms and optical illusions.

Around the corner from this museum, almost concealed in an unkempt inner courtyard at Fő tér 1 is the crumbling Zichy Villa, which houses the idiosyncratic **Kassák Museum** (Tues–Sun 10am–6pm, 5pm in winter; tel: 368 7021). Lajos Kassák, a poet, publisher, painter and political agitator, set out in 1909 to discover the world. He returned with the new political and artistic ideas that were engulfing western Europe. Cubism and Futurism influenced the form of his writing and also his cultural-political activities.

The main square, **Fő tér**, is distinctive for its old town hall and a row of attractive town houses. On the right is a smaller square in which stands a fascinating group of figures, *Women with Umbrellas*, by Imre Varga, the country's leading sculptor. (Other works by Varga that you might have encountered in your perambulations around the city include the Holocaust Memorial and the statue of Imre Nagy.)

Meet Imre Varga

Beyond this ensemble you will find the **Imre Varga Collection** (Tues–Sun 10am–6pm; tel: 250 0274) at Laktanya utca 7. Of particularly poignant interest is a row of highly decorated soldiers: they stand in their full finery, their proud medal-covered chests puffed out – but each has a wooden stump instead of a left leg. This mordant attack on militarism was very daring for an artist working under the yoke of communist rule. There are also some impressive pieces of sculpture in the garden. The collection's curators will be happy to furnish you with more detailed information on the life and work of this internationally acclaimed artist, who represented Hungary at the Venice Biennale in 1984. Varga himself sometimes puts in an appearance at the museum – often on Saturdays at lunch time – and chats with visitors for an hour or two.

If you're interested in ancient art, go to Szentendre út and cross it at the underpass. Turn right into Kerék út and left into Herkules utca to reach No 21 and the ruins of the **Hercules Villa**, which has some great mosaics. Back in Fő tér, **Sipos Halászkert** is a good lunch bet, especially for seafood.

Right: one of Varga's *Women with Umbrellas*

Larger than the Colosseum

Archaeology aficionados should now turn south to stroll through Óbuda. Here you will encounter the remains of the Roman town of *Aquincum*, dating back to the 1st century AD. Graceful columns stand in the lee of modern tower-block apartments, and you can see the ruins of a 16,000-seat **military amphitheatre** that was even larger than the Colosseum in Rome. Rather than walk to this site, you might board the HÉV at Árpád hid and travel back towards town for two stops to Szépvolgyi út: the amphitheatre is across the road from the station. Not far from the amphitheatre is Óbuda's former **synagogue** (Lajos utca 163), an imposing neoclassical building with a six-columned portico. It is now a television studio.

Also on Lajos utca, at No 168, is the **Óbuda Parish Church**, which was constructed in 1744–9 on the site of the Roman military camp. The interior contains a glorious carved pulpit showing the Good Shepherd and Mary Magdalene. Even if you are not utterly fascinated by ruins, you might want to travel one stop north from Árpád hid on the HÉV train and alight at Aquincum. Here stand the remains of the **civilian amphitheatre**. This was smaller than its military counterpart but its ruins are worth seeing. Across the road are the quite extensive remains of the Roman town (mid-Apr and Oct: Tues–Sun 9am–5pm; May–Sept Tues–Sun 9am–6pm; tel: 368 8241), which had a population of around 50,000 in its heyday. Stroll along its streets, viewing the outlines of temples, a market-hall, bathing establishments and houses. At the centre of the site a neoclassical **museum** displays items found at the location. Two of the most outstanding exhibits are a statue of Mithras and a water organ.

Above: Aquincum's neoclassical museum

7. JOZSEF NADOR SQUARE *(see map, p30)*

Cross the Chain Bridge to see the finest 19th-century Pest architecture.

To the start: take Metro M3 and alight at Vörösmarty tér.

Exit from the northeast corner of Vörösmarty tér (on the right side of Café Gerbeaud as you face it) and you will arrive in **József Nádor tér**. In the centre of this noisy, traffic-filled square lies a small park containing a mighty statue of the Archduke Joseph, who ruled Hungary for the first half of the 19th century. Also in the square note the neoclassical **Gross House**, which dates back to 1824. Next door is a shop that specialises in world-famous Herend porcelain. On the north side of the square check out **Derra House**, especially its finely restored facade. This building was originally constructed for a wealthy Greek merchant. Then turn left down J. Attila utca to arrive at Roosevelt tér, a park that leads to the Chain Bridge.

Gresham Palace, the second building on your right in **Roosevelt tér** (named after Franklin, not Theodore), was once the finest Art Nouveau building in Budapest. The London banking and insurance company that gave the palace its name moved into this building, designed by Zsigmond Quitter, in 1906, whereupon the palace's owner had himself immortalised in a larger-than-life relief. On sunny afternoons the facade lights up and the whole building is surrounded by a wonderful golden aura. Alas, the magnificent iron gates and the domed hall are the only real reminders of its former splendour. During the decades of communist rule the building fell into disrepair and when the new city council was unable to raise enough money for its restoration it was sold to foreign investors. Unfortunately the deal did not include clauses obliging the purchaser to improve its appearance, but the building is due to open as a Four Seasons hotel, by which time, locals hope, its once glorious appearance will have been restored.

Hungarian Scholars Society

The **Academy of Sciences** on the northern side of the square was founded in the mid-20th century and has a well-preserved neo-Renaissance exterior. A bronze relief on the wall facing Akadémia utca illustrates a significant event in the foundation of the academy: at the Reform Diet of 1825, Count István Széchenyi offered a year's income from his estates to establish a Hungarian Scholars Society. The count's monument is a surprisingly inconspicuous affair, located as it is in the small park in the middle of the square.

If you cross the **Chain Bridge** (Széchenyi lánchíd), built in 1860, to the Buda side of the city, you can either take the **Sikló funicular** for a further look at the castle and its museums *(see Itinerary 1, pages 23–4)* or stroll along the panoramic promenade that runs alongside the river. Turn left once you have crossed the river and, after more than 1km (½ mile), pass through the Tabán district, to the **Hotel Gellért**. Alternatively, a right turn soon leads to the district of **Viziváros** or **Water City**, which is explored in more detail in *The Danube and Király Baths, pages 41–2.*

Right: the István Széchenyi monument

8. MARGARET ISLAND *(see map, p44)*

A half-day walking tour on this tranquil island in the Danube, including a visit to the Palatinus Open-Air Thermal Swimming Baths. Round off the day with a fine dinner at the Danubius Grand Hotel.

To the start: No 26 bus from Marx tér. If you are travelling by car, turn south midway across the Árpád híd bridge.

Margaret Island in the Danube is situated between Margit híd to the south and Árpád híd to the north. A fertile spot 2½km (1½ miles) long and up to 500 metres/yds wide, it has shady parks, good swimming pools, romantic ruins, attractive cafés and elegant hotel-restaurants: just the place for a summer's

day. Despite its urban setting, the island is an oasis of tranquillity. Private cars are banned: see under 'Island Attractions' below for how to get around.

The Romans, the first to take advantage of its springs, established a park, a thermal bath and a fortress. Centuries later King Béla IV (1235–70) settled several religious orders here. These included a group of Dominican nuns, to whom he entrusted his beloved daughter, Margit (Margaret). The ruins and indeed the island's name date from that time. Here, too, the Turkish pasha entrusted the ladies from his harem to eunuchs; this 'island of women' thus developed a legendary reputation in Christian Europe. 'Palatin' archduke Joseph used the site for his summer residence, and he had the botanical gardens laid out in 1796. His son Rudolf restored the Roman tradition of the thermal bath. After World War I, the island was declared a free public park.

Island Attractions

The island features a choice of fun transport to hire, especially at **Bringóvár** (Bike Castle) at the northern end. These include pedal cars, electric cars, four-wheel cycles, horse-drawn carriages and a tractor-train. In the centre of the island is a well tended park with the medieval ruins of the **Franciscan church** and the **Dominican nuns church and convent**. On the western side, the **Palatinus Thermal Baths** have extensive open-air pools (including a wave pool); nude sunbathing is allowed on the single-sex terraces.

To the north, below the 57-metre (190-ft) high **water-tower**, which you can ascend, is the **open-air theatre** which stages operas and concerts on a regular basis. The **Thermal Hotel**, with therapeutic baths open to the public, towers above the island's northeastern point: next door is the stylish **Grand Hotel** with its recommended restaurants and café. Nearby is a **Japanese Water Garden**. Note that you can drive to the hotels via the Árpád Bridge.

Above: Margaret Island's Palatinus Baths. **Right:** a monument to Soviet-Hungarian friendship at the entrance to Statue Park. **Following Page:** the opera house

9. STATUE PARK   *(see pull-out map)*

Massive memorials commemorating the dark days of communism.

To the start: No 7 bus (blue) to Kostolányi Dezsö tér, then the Volán bus (yellow), departing from platform 6.

What is a country to do with the symbols of a hated totalitarian regime when the oppressors are overthrown? In most cases it is not long before the statues and edifices that honour the regime are overturned and destroyed amid scenes of joyous celebration. (The Berlin Wall for example was spontaneously deconstructed by individuals who used their bare hands to rid themselves of the structure, brick by brick.) Conversely, no matter how much a society wants to forget reminders of a painful past, the obliteration of historic truths does not have a place in a modern democracy. Such was the dilemma that faced Hungary when Soviet hegemony fell apart in 1989.

Blasts from the Past

The issue was resolved by the establishment of a statue park in the southwest of Budapest. The park opened in the autumn of 1993 with 41 works that had previously stood in prominent positions throughout the city. A niche at one side of a monumental pseudo-classical red-brick entrance to the park houses a statue of Lenin; on the other side is a Cubist-style carving of Marx and Engels. Revolutionary music blares out of a ticket office (mid-Mar–mid-Nov 10am–dusk; tel: 227 7446), from which you can also buy drinks with names such as Molotov cocktails, and kitsch items ranging from Marx T-shirts to cans of 'the last breath of socialism'.

Gigantic statues of pre-World War II Hungarian communists and assorted Soviet heroes are arranged in six groups. A fierce, flag-waving soldier based on a call-to-arms poster issued by the communist government in 1919 typifies the chunky totalitarian style favoured by Soviet aesthetes. This statue was moved from its former position at the foot of the Liberation monument on Gellérthegy. Less imposing but quite evocative is the monument depicting the 1919 Hungarian revolution leader Béla Kun urging a crowd of soldiers and workers on towards the dictatorship of the proletariat. Given the nature of communist ideology, it's not surprising that some statues commemorate groups, such as Spanish Civil War martyrs, rather than individuals.

city itineraries

10. ALONG ANDRÁSSY ÚT   *(see map below)*

Stroll along Andrássy út to the Millennium Monument on Heroes' Square, and visit the square's two fine galleries. Lunch at the world-famous Gundel restaurant and ride back to your accommodation on continental Europe's oldest underground railway.

To the start: all Metro lines go to Deák tér where you should alight.

Deák tér is one of the busiest squares in Budapest, not least because the city's three Metro lines intersect here. From the square you will see the cupola of

the neo-Romanesque **St Stephen's Basilica** about 300 metres/yds to the north. You should make for it.

Everybody calls St Stephen's a 'basilica' even though the architecture isn't exactly reminiscent of Roman styles. During its construction in 1868, the mighty dome, almost 100 metres/330ft high, collapsed due to faulty structural planning, and it was only in 1906 that this church, which has room for almost 9,000 people, could finally be consecrated. A steady stream of Hungarian Catholics (75 percent of the country's population is Catholic) make the pilgrimage to see the right hand of St Stephen, a relic with a chapel all to itself. The cupola may be ascended (10am–6pm) for a view of the city from a height of 65 metres (217ft), but not if you don't fancy a steep climb. The elevator covers the major part of the ascent but then it is a slog up 137 spiral stairs.

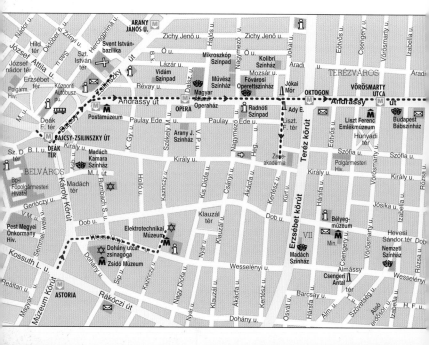

After this brief detour walk to the rear of the church to reach Bajcsy-Zsilinszky út and then immediately turn left to enter Andrássy út. After the advantageous 'Compromise' with Austria, many felt that the time had come to turn the town planners' vision of a proper connection between the City Park and the Chain Bridge into reality. The idea was to mark the country's millennial festivities by unveiling a heroic statue at the end of the new road. By 1886, 10 years before the 1,000th anniversary, the new road had been largely completed. Even today, its buildings convey a strong stylistic unity.

Mahler's Debut

The lower section of the street is narrow, but the tree-shaded pavements are a good place for a stroll, and shopaholics should appreciate the neighbourhood's many specialist shops. Soon you'll reach the **Opera House** on the left, an impressive building dating from 1884 (daily 45-minute tours take place at 3pm and 4pm; you may be able to get opera tickets from the daytime box office (10am–7pm, tel: 331 2550) at the left of the building, but a safer bet is to order in advance from the central ticket office at Andrássy út 15, tel: 267 9737). The facade is richly ornamented and the building can house 1,300 beneath its broad dome. This is where Gustav Mahler made his youthful debut as chief conductor, and where Puccini supervised the first performance of *Madame Butterfly*. The great conductor Otto Klemperer restored the Opera House's international reputation in 1947–1950.

Opposite the Opera House is the Palais Drechsler, built by Ödön Lechner. Though Lechner is known as an exponent of Art Nouveau, for his work on the palais, he kept to the guidelines of Opera House architect Miklós Ybl, and created a purely neoclassical building. Until recently the palais housed the School of Ballet, but it is currently being redeveloped as a hotel. Just beyond the palais, at No 29, is the **Muvész** coffee-house, where many of

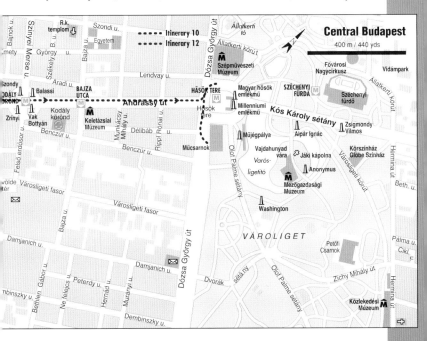

the city's Bohemian types gather early on weekday mornings. A good alternative to morning coffee here is to wait for 20 minutes until you come to **Lukács**, a handsome traditional coffee house at No 70.

The major intersection of Andrássy út and **Nagymezö utca** is 200 metres/yds beyond the Muvész coffee house. Locals call Nagymezö utca 'Broadway' because it is full of cinemas, theatres and nightclubs. Another 200 metres/yds beyond this intersection, on the right of Andrássy út, you will find **Liszt Ferenc tér**. The statue here is not of the composer but of the poet Endre Ady; another poet, Mór Jókai, is immortalised in stone on the other side of Andrássy út. As for Franz Liszt, he hardly spoke a word of Hungarian after a career in France, Austria and Germany, but he remains the country's most illustrious name in the world of music, and you can see his statue deeper into the square named after him. Beyond, on the left of the square, is the Art Nouveau **Academy of Music**, whose exotically decorated halls are open to visitors. To see more examples of Art Nouveau, exit from Liszt Ferenc tér into Paulay Ede utca and you can't miss the small but delightful **Új Színház** (New Theatre), which opened in 1905.

At Home With Liszt

After this brief detour return to Andrássy út. After a few steps you will be in the **Octagon**, through which the **Outer Ring Road** (Teréz körút) runs. From here the road becomes wider. Liszt lived in the neo-Renaissance house at No 67 – look out for bas reliefs of J.S. Bach, Mozart, Beethoven, Erkel, Haydn and Liszt over the second floor windows. Bach established an Academy of Music on the site, which is now a museum (Mon–Fri 10am–6pm, Sat 10am–5pm; tel: 343 0565).

Above: ceiling frescoes by Lotz, National Museum
Right: standing to attention on Heroes' Square

You will soon arrive at the **Kodály körönd** (circular flower-bed). The splendour of the apartments around this circle has faded but the shaded beer-garden to the left is still a pleasant place in which to sit. Further along Andrássy út gardens appear in front of the various facades, which include some neo-Renaissance and Secessionist-style villas.

Continue to the end of the avenue, where **Heroes' Square** is dominated by the **Millennium Monument**, erected in 1896 to mark the '1,000-year celebration of the Magyar occupation of the homeland'. At the top of the high column the Archangel Gabriel hands his crown to King Stephen I, founder of the state, in accordance with the myth relating to the country's foundation. Immortalised in stone at the foot of the statue are the seven legendary tribal chieftains who took part in the original Magyar conquest. This gigantic monument to Hungarian national pride is flanked by two colonnades featuring allegorical depictions of war and peace and statues of national heroes.

The enormous square is framed by two museums. The **Palace of Art** (Tues–Sun 10am–6pm; tel: 343 7401) on the right was opened in 1896. For many years this gallery would have nothing to do with modern art, but it has long since shed such conservatism and today it features some fascinating exhibitions, films and performances. The monumental **Museum of Fine Arts** (Tues–Sun 10am–5.30pm; tel: 343 9757) on the left provides an impressive documentation of art history ranging from the artefacts in its Ancient Egyptian department to modern paintings.

Of particular note are canvases by Brueghel the Elder and the Spanish school – El Greco, Murillo, Goya and Velazquez.

Hungarian Cuisine

Before visiting these museums you might wish to have lunch in one of the vicinity's two quite excellent restaurants. The traditional **Gundel** (Állatkerti körút 2, tel: 321 3550), behind the Fine Arts Museum, was established by János Gundel, founder of an eminent dynasty of cooks. It was taken over in 1910 by his son Károly, who is credited as being the founding father of Hungarian *nouvelle cuisine*. From noon until midnight, exquisite delicacies are served in the magnificent garden or in the dining-room. A classic Gundel menu dating from 1912 begins with *palatsch* soup, followed by *perche à la maison*. The recommended main course is *fricassée* of beef on mimosa salad, with *crêpes à la Gundel* to finish off. Today, such a meal will cost around 6,000 forints; the menu displayed in the old foyer reveals that prices were somewhat lower in the years before World War I. Alternatively, for a taste of Gundel's but at more affordable prices, you might wish to try its neighbour, Bagolyvár (Állatkerti körút 2, tel: 343 0217).

Return to the city on the M1 Metro line, which is the oldest underground line in continental Europe. Like much of Budapest's architecture and many of its attractions, it was opened in 1896 for the millennium celebrations.

Above: exhibit in the Old Masters Gallery, Museum of Fine Arts

11. CITY PARK *(see map, p48–9)*

Urban greenery that has something for everyone.

To the start: take Metro M1 and alight at Hösök tér.

Behind the Millennium Monument spreads **City Park** (Városliget), built in 1896. In its 1-sq-km area you will find lots of shaded lawns, and any number of attractions. On Állatkerti körút, to the left of the monument and beyond the Museum of Fine Arts are the **Zoo** (9am–4, 5, 6 or 7pm depending on the month; tel: 343 6882), an **amusement park** (Oct–Mar 10am–6pm, Apr–Sept 10am–8pm; tel: 343 9810) and a **circus** (Nov–Aug: Wed–Sun 10am, 7pm; tel: 343 9630).

Aquatic Chess

Adjacent to the zoo is **Gundel**, Hungary's most famous restaurant *(see page 51)*, and opposite the circus are the **Széchenyi Thermal Baths** (tel: 321 0310, *see page 40*). The recently renovated baths have enormous outdoor pools in which much of the city's male population seems to spend its time playing chess.

Directly behind the monument, in Heroes' Square, a bridge crosses the park's lake which is used for skating in winter and boating in summer. You can see the hotchpotch of architectural styles that is **Vajdahunyad Castle** to the right. The castle was built as a temporary structure in 1896 but proved so popular that it was replaced by a permanent structure. Part of it houses the largest **Agricultural Museum** (Mar–mid-Nov: Tues–Sun 10am–5pm; mid-Nov–Feb: Tues–Sun 10am–4pm; tel: 343 0573) in Europe.

The eastern end of the park is home to the **Transport Museum** (Oct–Apr: Tues–Sun 10am–4pm; May–Sept: Tues–Sun 10am–5pm; tel: 343 0565). Here also is the **Petőfi Csarnok** youth entertainment centre. Rock bands often perform in the centre's cavernous hall, or outdoors if the weather allows. At weekends it is the site of a flea market *(see page 64–65)*.

12. JEWISH BUDAPEST *(see map, p48–9)*

A visit to the quarter of the city beyond the Inner Ring Road and north of Rákóczi út, with its small Jewish community and large synagogue.

To the start: take Metro M2 and alight at Astoria.

On emerging from the Metro, walk for one block on Károly Körút and arrive, at the junction of **Dohány** and **Wésselenyi utca**, at the Great Synagogue. Since the early days of the city's history, Budapest's Jewish community has made a major contribution to its development. Indeed in the closing years of the 19th century more than one-quarter of the city's population was Jewish. In contrast with their treatment elsewhere in Europe, Jews were accepted as Hungarians of Jewish faith, and there was never a time when they were forced to live in ghettoes. All this changed in the 20th century. In the 1930s Admiral Horthy's regime fostered ties with Nazi Germany and fascist Italy, and in 1944 the Nazis invaded the country. Though Horthy belatedly dissociated himself from Hitler, hundreds of thousands of Hungary's Jews were either killed by Arrow Cross fascists or sent to their deaths in Nazi concentration camps. Some 80,000 Jews now live in Hungary, mostly in Budapest.

Klezmer Concerts

The **Great Synagogue** (Mon–Fri 10am–3pm, Sun 10am–1pm)was built in the 1850s in Byzantine-Moorish style, with two striking onion-domed 'minarets'. The largest synagogue in Europe, it can accommodate up to 3,000 worshippers. The interior has three naves, and separate galleries for women. Concerts here utilise the magnificent organ, and this is also a good place to hear ethnic klezmer (clarinet) music. The synagogue has a **Jewish Museum** featuring artefacts from ancient Rome to the present. One room, draped in black, documents the Holocaust.

On leaving turn the corner into Wesslényi utca for the **Raoul Wallenberg Memorial Garden** (same opening hours as Great Synagogue) named after the Swedish consul who saved 20,000 Jews from the Nazis. The centrepiece of the park is Imre Varga's *Weeping Willow,* with the names of some of the hundreds of thousands of victims killed by the Nazis engraved into its leaves.

Continue north on Wesslényi utca and turn left at Kazinczy utca. On the curve of this street is the **Orthodox Synagogue**, an Art Nouveau building with a Hebrew inscription on its pediment that reads: 'This place is none other than the house of God and the place to heaven.' The synagogue is not open to visitors but you can peer through a window to see the interior. A gate at the right leads into a courtyard, where there is a Jewish school and the ultrakosher **Hanna** restaurant. Next door, at No 31, is the pleasant non-kosher Jewish **Carmel** restaurant.

Above Left: a big attraction at the zoo. **Left:** chess, a popular pastime at the Széchenyi Thermal Baths. **Right:** stained-glass window in the Jewish Museum

Excursions

1. SZENTENDRE   *(see map, p60)*

A half- or full-day's excursion to the north of Budapest, to Szentendre (St Andrew) on a bend in the Danube River. This small, attractive town, the centre of Serbian settlement in Hungary, has been renowned as an artists' colony since the early 1920s, and is now a tourist centre.

There is a suburban train (HÉV) from Batthyány to Szentendre every 10 to 30 minutes. The journey takes 45 minutes. Volánbusz buses leave Árpad hid bus terminal for Szentendre every 30 minutes; the journey time is 30 minutes. In Szentendre the train and bus stations are next to each other. Disembark, take the underpass and emerge on Kossuth Lajos utca which, after 1km (½ a mile) leads, via Dumtsa Jenő utca, to Főtér, the centre of Szentendre.

Alternatively, board a boat at V. Vigadó tér at 9am or 2pm. Return boats leave Szentendre at 11.45am, 5.15pm and, in the summer months, at 6.15pm. The outward voyage takes 100 minutes; the return voyage 75 minutes. You can reserve lunch places at Aranysárkány (noon–10pm, tel 311 670).

En route into the town you will pass, just before the tourist office, the first evidence of Serbian presence in Szentendre. The **Pozarevacka church**, built in 1773, has a wonderful icon wall in Byzantine style. A couple of hundred metres further is **Fő tér**, an irregular space that constitutes the heart of Szentendre. Its centrepiece, the **Plague Monument**, a masterpiece of wrought-iron work, was erected in 1763 as a token of thanksgiving after the town was spared from the plague that ravaged the surrounding countryside.

Three Art Museums

Immediately behind Fő tér, three quite exceptional galleries beckon. An 18th-century building (Apr–Oct: Tues–Sun 10am–6pm; Nov–Mar: 10am–4pm; tel: 310 244) that was originally a salt depot houses the works of **Margít Kovács**, Hungary's best known ceramic artist. Her naive figures were dismissed by critics but won greater acclaim with the public. In the nearby **Ferenczy Museum** (Wed–Sun 10am–4pm; tel: 310 244), which was built as a Serbian school more than 200 years ago, the collected works of the entire Ferenczy family are spread over four spacious floors. Károly Ferenczy, the patriarch, was one of Hungary's leading impressionists.

The **Ámos and Anna Museum** (Fri–Sun 10am–4pm) contains the works of the lyrical painter Ámos Imre and his wife, Anna Margít, who was a surrealist. Just past the museum you can see the output of today's Szentendre artists in the **Muvészet Malom** (Art Mill 10am–6pm; tel: 319 128), an exhibition hall which has been created from an old sawmill.

Left: Szentendre has been an artists' colony since the 1920s
Right: the Church of St John is the town's oldest building

An enjoyable place for a coffee break and, in season, delicious chocolate-coated chestnut sweetmeats, is the nearby **Incognito** on Bogdányi utca. For lunch or dinner, the **Aranysárkány Vendélgö** on Alkotamány utca serves delicious Hungarian food and has an excellent wine list. This was the first restaurant in the country to be privatised after the communist regime fell.

There is little need to worry about further directions around a town built on a gently inclining hillside that slopes down to the Danube. Wander the cobbled streets, where the only traffic is an occasional horse-drawn carriage, and enjoy the host of shops and stalls selling folk art and rather splendid glass. At some point you might stroll down to the Danube embankment, from where you can watch life pass slowly by on the river.

On the southern side of Fő tér, adjacent to the Ferency Museum, you will find the only Serbian church certain to be open – the tiny **Blagovestenska church** (Tues–Sun 10am–5pm), built in 1754. The choral voices inside are recorded rather than live but are delightful nevertheless. Look out for the rococo iconostasis of carved limewood, and the elaborate 18th-century furnishings.

Belgrade Cathedral

If you wander up the winding cobbled streets to **Templom tér**, you can catch wonderful views over the town. Here stands the parish **Church of St John** (Tues–Sun 10am–6pm), the oldest building in Szentendre. Although reconstructed in baroque style in the 18th century, the church retains a number of visible traces of its medieval heritage. From Templom tér, you can't miss the blood-red tower of **Belgrade Cathedral**. Surrounded by tall trees and a wall, the cathedral is open only for Sunday service (10am). There is, however, one building in the leafy compound that is bound to be open: the **Serbian Ecclesiastical Art Collection** (Tues–Sun 10am–6pm) features a treasure trove of icons, liturgical vessels and Arabic scrolls dating from the Ottoman period.

The **Hungarian Open-Air Ethnographical Museum** (Tues–Sun 9am–5pm; tel: 312 304) is not yet finished but is well worth visiting. The museum is situated some 3km (2 miles) from Szentendre and can be reached by bus (one every hour) from platform 8 of the bus station. The idea behind the museum is to gather buildings – churches, farmhouses, windmills, and so forth – from 10 diverse regions of the country to illustrate multifaceted features of Hungarian life over the course of three centuries. Until now, buildings from only four regions have been gathered, of which arguably the most interesting is the 17th-century Greek Orthodox church from the village of Mándok near Zahony on the Ukrainian border.

Above: view over the rooftops of Szentendre

2. EGER *(see map, p60)*

Eger, situated 128km (80 miles) northeast of Budapest, is a town with beautiful baroque architecture, and more listed buildings than anywhere else in Hungary, Budapest and Sopron notwithstanding. Another of Eger's claims to fame is that it is the home of Bull's Blood wine.

Several trains depart from Keleti station every day. The best option is to board an inter-city train which makes the journey in just under two hours. Change trains at Füzesabony. On arriving at Eger railway station, walk up the short stretch to the main road, Somogyi Béla utca, turn right and, after about 10 minutes, you will arrive in the heart of the pedestrianised town.

On reaching the town centre, you will notice the cream-coloured twin towers and dome of the massive **cathedral** (6am–7pm). This, the country's second-largest church – only Esztergom's cathedral is bigger – was built in the 1830s from the neoclassical design of József Hild, who designed the Esztergom cathedral. Enter via a monumental staircase, and notice the crucifix-brandishing statues of Faith, Hope and Charity which crown the pediment.

More Twin Towers

From the cathedral make your way into the pedestrianised area and stroll through the shopping streets to **Dobo Istvan tér**, the grand square that constitutes Eger's focal point. (Generous signposting indicates the route.) Looming over the square are the twin towers of the **Minorite church**, a magnificent baroque structure dating from 1773. The church alterpiece of the Virgin Mary and St Anthony (its patron saints) is by the Bohemian painter Johan Lukas Kracker. In the square stand two statues by the renowned sculptor Zsigmond Kisfaludi Strobl: the one of **István Dobó** is flanked by

Above: Eger is full of beautiful baroque architecture.
Left: Strobl's statue of István Dobó

a knight and a woman; the other, *The Battles of the Border Forts*, depicts Turks, Hungarians and three horses locked in mortal combat.

The ruins of the **castle** (9am–5, 6 or 7pm depending on the season; the casemates are open daily, 8am–8pm in summer, shorter hours in winter) dominate the square's northeastern aspect and offer wonderful views of the city. The castle was built in 1271 after the Mongol invasion and proved its worth in 1552 when some 2,000 Hungarians managed to keep at bay an overwhelming force of 100,000 Turks. This valiant act of resistance is recalled by exhibitions in the Heroes' Hall of the **István**

Dobó Museum (Tues–Sun 8am–5pm), which occupies the former Bishop's Palace within the fortress complex. Pride of place is given to a statue of Dobó himself. The **Eger Art Gallery** (Tues–Sun 8am–5pm) contains portraits of eminent Hungarians and several works by Mihály Munkácsy, the undisputed master of the folk genre.

A short distance to the west of the castle, at the corner of Knézich utca and Markó Ferenc utca, stands a reminder of the Turks: a slender, 14-sided, 34-metre (110ft)-tall **minaret**, whose mosque was destroyed in 1841. You can climb up the steps – if the attendant is absent ask at the Minaret Hotel across the road – for great vistas of Eger and the surrounding countryside.

Retrace your steps and opposite the cathedral you will see the huge, undistinguished-looking **Lyceum School**, founded by Károly Eszterházy, a bishop of Eger. On the first floor of the south wing, check out the library (summer: Tues–Fri 9.30am–3.30pm, Sat, Sun 9.30am–12.30pm; winter: Tues–Fri 9.30am–12.30pm, Sat, Sun 9.30am–noon) with its glorious baroque carved bookshelves. The highlight is the 1778 library ceiling fresco by Kracker and József Zach. A masterpiece of Hungarian art, it depicts the Council of Trent (1543–63) complete with a lightning bolt setting the council's heretical (Protestant) manuscripts ablaze. Ascend to the observatory on the sixth floor, which contains 18th-century astronomical equipment, then press on upwards for a further three floors to see great views of Eger and the surrounding countryside.

Bull's Blood

If you're in the mood for some refreshment, this is wine country, and the home of the traditional Bull's Blood brand. Make your way by taxi or on foot to **Szépasszony-völgy**, the Valley of Beautiful Women, which is about 3km (2 miles) from the town centre. Here, around a horse-shoe shaped green, dozens of wine cellars are cut deep into solid rock. Wine is cheap through-

Above: a viticultural paradise. **Left:** in the Valley of Beautiful Women. **Right:** the cogwheel railway

out Hungary, and if the prices advertised by some cellars seem high, bear in mind that you're looking at the cost (about $1.50) not of a glass but of a bottle. Wine by the glass is so inexpensive that it's tempting to keep drinking until you wind up inebriated. The cellars attract groups of natives for the local equivalent to bingo or theatre evenings – and an accordion player or a fiddler will invariably produce some folk tunes. After sampling the wines these happy groups often adjourn to the green for a barbecue.

You might want to forego the pleasures of the grape for a visit to the **strand** – a large outdoor complex of swimming pools – or to the adjacent **thermal baths** 500 metres/yds east of the town centre. The **Fehér Szarvas Vadásztanya** (White Stag Hunting Inn) is a good spot for dinner, as is the **Senátor Ház**, which also does fine lunches. The former offers a full range of Hungarian wild-game specialities and outstanding regional wines, while the latter is more basic. If you plan an overnight stay, the Senátor Ház (tel: 36 320 466) is a charming 18th-century inn with 11 bedrooms.

3. THROUGH THE BUDA HILLS BY TRAIN *(see map, p60)*

Take a ride on several idiosyncratic forms of transport to travel through the Buda Hills, enjoying the passing scenery as you go. On this excursion it is not the destination but the journey itself that matters.

To the start: At Moszkva tér board tram No 18 or bus No 56 for two stops and alight at the tall, circular Budapest Hotel. Cross the road to Városmajor, the terminal of the cogwheel railway.

Climb aboard the **Cogwheel Railway** (Fogaskereku), which runs at about 15-minute intervals, for a pleasant 20-minute journey through one of the most picturesque residential areas in Budapest. The railway might not look like the 21st-century train networks of some modern cities but it is a vital means of transport to numerous local commuters. Built in 1874, it stops at seven stations before reaching the terminal. The track covers 3.5km (2 miles) from Városemajor to **Széchenyi-hegy** (Széchenyi Hill) in the course of which it climbs to a height of 465 metres (1,550ft).

The Children's Railway

On leaving the cogwheel terminus turn left; on the right is a café where you might wish to stop for refreshments. A short distance after the café the terminus of the Children's Railway, some 600 metres from the cogwheel railway, comes into view. The **Children's Railway** (Gyermek Vasút), formerly the Pioneer Railway run by the Communist Youth Organisation, was constructed between 1948 and 1951. Virtually all of its staff – comptrollers, conductors, booking clerks – are children dressed in official MAV (Hungarian State Railway) uniforms. The youngsters receive special training and are supervised by adults. (You might be relieved to know that the engine driver is an adult.)

At the station you will find a train with open-sided carriages – if not, one will soon appear: the trains run throughout the day (Mondays excepted) on the hour, or there-abouts. Purchase your ticket at the station; it will be checked on the train by young conductors who also sell postcards that feature the railway. The train chugs its way for some 12km (8 miles) along the narrow-gauge track that follows the ridge of the Buda hills. The entire journey, during which there are seven stops, takes about 45 minutes.

The first stop is **Normafa**, which derives its name from an occasion in 1840 when a celebrated diva, Rozália Klein, sang the grand aria from Bellini's *Norma* to a company of artists seated under a large beech tree. Where the tree once stood there is now a plaque commemorating that alfresco rendition. Rather than proceeding to the end of the line you might wish to alight at the fourth stop – **János-hegy**. From here, a rather steep but fairly short (1km/½ mile) footpath leads to the **János-hegy Kilátó** (lookout), which is the highest point (529 metres/1,800ft) in Budapest. En route, the path crosses a macadam road at the side of which is a restaurant and the cable-car terminal.

The summit of János-hegy is topped by the 23.5-metre (80-ft) high neo-Romanesque **Erszébet Kilátó** (lookout tower), which dates back to 1910. Ascend this *kilátó* and you will be rewarded with sweeping panoramic views of the hills around Buda – in clear weather you can see as far as the Pilis hills to the north. Moreover, if you walk around the tower, you will gain a virtually comprehensive view of the city.

Once you have had your fill of the vistas, walk back the 400 metres (1,300ft) to the **chair lift** *(libego)* (closed on alternate Mondays) terminal that you previously passed. The open seats of the chair lift offer delightful views and provide a breezy journey down to the **Zugliget** (Hidden Woods), from where it is but a couple of hundred metres/yds to the stop for the No.158 bus, which will return you to your starting point on Moszkva tér.

Above: serious fun on the Children's Railway
Right: don't worry – the driver is an adult

If you are not inclined to make the climb to the Erszébet Lookout, or if you do not appreciate the windswept delights of chair lifts, you could stay on the Children's Railway until the end of the route at **Huvösvölgy** (Cool Valley) – a remarkably splendid station for such a small railway. From here it is but a short stroll down a flight of steps to the terminal from which you can board the No. 56 bus back to Moszkva tér.

Full Steam Ahead

In the summer months there's a treat in store for aficionados of historic rail travel. From May to September, the *Nostalgia*, a steam-powered train, puffs its way round the Danube bend on the first Saturday of each month. It departs Nuyugati Station for Esztergom at 9.50am, and sets out on the return journey at 4.25pm, thereby affording the visitor ample time in which to explore this historic town. On the other three Saturdays of these months the train travels to Nagymarls-Visegrad. The *Nostalgia* pulls four carriages, complete with the original-style wooden seats, a children's play carriage and the Dreher buffet carriage. For information, call 397 5392.

Railway buffs might also want to visit **Vasúti Emlékpark** (Historic Rail Park, Tatai út 95, mid-July–Oct: Mon–Fri 8am–4pm, Sat, Sun 10am–5pm; tel: 302 3580) which features about 100 museum pieces, many of which are still pressed into service as *Nostalgia* trains.

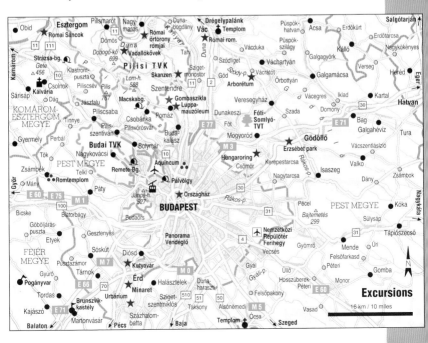

Leisure
Activities

SHOPPING

Most shops are open Mon–Fri 10am–6pm, Sat 9am–1pm; some close at 8pm on Thurs. Most shopping malls are also open Sun from 10am to anywhere between 4pm and 6pm.

On purchases of over 50,000 forints, you are entitled to refunds on the 25 percent VAT that is included in all prices. Look for stores with a Tax-Free logo in the window.

Antiques

Antiques shops selling jewellery, paintings, ceramics, bric-a-brac and furniture abound, especially at the upper section of Váci utca; Falk Miska utca and, at its northern end, around the corner to the left, Szent István körút; Fortuna út; Ferenciek tere and adjacent Kossuth Lajos utca; and at the east end of Castle Hill.

BÁV pawn and second-hand shops are at Andrássy út 27 and 43 *(objets d'art)*; Hess András tér 1 (porcelain, folk art); István krt. 3 (porcelain, textiles). BÁV auctions are held at Lónyai utca 30–32 (tel: 455 7700).

Auctions are also held at:

Gallery Keiselbach
Svent István körút 5
Tel: 269 3148

Belvárosi Aukciósház
Váci utca 36
Tel: 266 8374

Nagházi Gakéria és Aukciósház
Falk Miksa utca 13
Tel: 312 5631

Polgár Galéria és Aukciósház
Váci utca 11/b
Tel: 267 4077
Kossuth Lajos utca 3
Tel: 318 6954

Art Galleries

Galéria XXI
Váci utca 59; tel: 267 5445
Varied works, mainly collages, by the owner, István Horkay.

Left: Fishermen's Bastion restaurant
Right: souvenir time

Gallery Kieselbach
Szent István körút 5; tel: 269 3148
Continually changing displays of avant-garde Hungarian works, plus paintings from elsewhere in Europe.

Haas Galéria
Falk Miksa utca 13; tel: 332 3253
Specialising in 20th-century Hungarian art.

Mednyánszky Galéria
Károly körút 26; tel: 317 5983
Contemporary works of Hungarian fine and applied art.

Mügyüjtök Galériéja (Collectors' Gallery)
Kossuth Lagos utca 10; tel: 317 5995
Hungarian and European paintings and drawings from the 19th and 20th centuries.

Rósza Galéria
Szentháromság utca 15; tel: 355 6866
Castle Hill outlet for contemporary Hungarian artists.

Sziget Galéria
Váci utca 63; tel: 266 6549
A good selection of 19th- and 20th-century and contemporary paintings.

Varfok Galéria
Várfok utca 14; tel: 213 5155
Gallery off Moszkva tér showing the work of young Hungarian artists.

Books

Bestsellers
Október 6 utca 11; tel: 312 1295
New English-language books every week.

Corvina
Vörösmarty tér 1 (2nd floor, Room 201);
tel: 317 5185
Founded by the state to bring Hungarian literature (in translation) to the world.

Király Books
Fő utca 79; tel: 214 0972
Two floors of English and French books.

Libri Könyvpalota
Rákóczi út 12; tel: 267 4844
Vast new local version of Borders bookshop.

Libri Studium
Váci utca 22; tel: 318 5680
English-language travel guides, maps.

Litéa
Hess András tér 4; tel: 375 4385
Delightful store with lots of travel guides and foreign-language books, and a teahouse.

Párisi Udvar
Petőfi Sándor utca 2 (in arcade)
tel: 318 3136
Wide selection of travel books, maps, CDs, Hungarian literature in translation.

Ceramics

Haas & Czjzek
Bajcsy-Zsilinszky út 23; tel: 311 4094
Comprehensive range of Hungarian pottery.

Herend
József Nádor tér 11; tel: 267 4826/317 2622
Glorious ceramics from western Hungary. Also at Kigyó 5 (tel: 318 3439) which offers shipping and on Castle Hill at Szentháromság 5 (tel: 375 5857).

Herend Village Pottery
Váci utca 23; tel: 318 2094
Sturdy kitchen pottery, Herend porcelain.

Zsolnay
Kigyó utca 4; tel 318 3712
Art Nouveau tiles from famous Péc factory.

Fashion

Clara Lisk
Váci utca 12; tel: 267 2728
Upmarket ladies clothing, including fur coats.

Jackpot and Cottonfield
Téréz körút 24; tel: 266 0221
Scandinavian casual wear for men, women.

Eduard Kettner
Andrássy út 21; tel: 351 0300
Great collection for field sports enthusiasts.

Kleider Bauer
Váci utca 17; tel: 318 3337
Exclusive men's branch of a 20-store chain.

Luxus Department Store
Vörösmarty tér; tel: 318 3355
Last of the stately old-time clothing stores; three floors of Europe's top names in men's and women's fashions and accessories.

Manier
Váci utca 53; tel: 318 1292
One-off and ready to wear moderately priced funky garments by a Hungarian designer.

Monarchia
Szabad sajtó út 6; tel: 318 3146
Chic women's suits and daring gowns by local designers. One-off, made-to-measure.

Sixvil Fashion Store and Café
Kecskeméti utca 8; tel: 317 4834
Men's, women's items by top local designers

Tango Classic
Apáczai Csere János utca 3; tel: 318 4394
Exclusive handmade clothing for women, made to measure by Hungarian designers.

Zilli
Kempinski Hotel
1052 Erzsébet tér 7–8; tel: 429 3884
Exclusive luxury men's tailors, couturiers.

Flea Markets

Józsefvárosi (Chinese) Market
Kobányai út 21–31
Daily 7am–4pm.
The closest flea market to the city centre (tram 28 or 36), and by far the largest.

Right: Hungarian dolls are less famous than their Russian counterparts but make fine gifts

Ecseri Market
Nagykörösi út 156 (bus 54 from Bóraros tér)
Mon–Fri 8am–4pm, Sat 7am–3pm
It's quite a trek to this, the city's most famous antiques market, but it's good for textiles, folk costumes, communist memorabilia; early Sat for best buys.

Petöfi Csarnock (Városligeti) Market
Zichy Mihály út (Metro M1 to Széchenyi fürdö)
Sat, Sun 7am–2pm
The smallest City Park market; pleasant to visit but not much of interest on sale.

Folk Art
Central Market Hall
Vámház körút 1–3; tel: 117 6865
The second floor of this market has lots of stalls with a wide selection of folk-art items.

Folkart Centrum
Váci utca 14; tel: 318 5840
also Rákóci út 32; tel: 342 753
A large state-owned store that stocks good-quality Magyar kitsch at reasonable prices.

Holló Folk Art
Vitkovics Mihály utca 12; tel: 317 8103
Handicraft reproductions of diverse folk-art items from various regions; particularly good for decorative boxes, traditional pottery, wooden candlesticks.

Vali Folklór
Váci utca 23; tel: 337 6301
A crammed, tiny shop situated in a small courtyard that sells second-hand traditional clothing, ceramics and hand-carved wooden items. Occasional genuine Russian icons.

Malls & Arcades
Of the 12 modern malls in the city, the following two are particularly good for clothes.

Millennium Centre
Váci utca 19–21
Fairly new arcade mainly devoted to designer shops.

Westend City Center
Vaci út
Handsome, large, up-market mall near Nyugati railway station with about 400 stores.

Markets
Central Market Hall
Vámház körút 1–3; tel: 117 6865
Mon–Thurs 6am–4pm, Fri 6am–7pm, Sat 6am–3pm
Situated on the Pest side of the Freedom Bridge, this hall – a gem of late 19th-century architecture – is worth a visit if only for its picturesque stalls and lively atmosphere – and for a snack.

Other weekly markets stock produce from the countryside. Many stallholders sell their own produce. The following are open weekdays 6am–6pm:
Hold utca in district V in northern Pest
Bosnyák tér in district XIV in northeast Pest
Fény utca near Moszkva tér in the northwest of Buda.

The following are also open Sun 6am–1pm:
Batthyány tér 2–6 in Buda at the exit from the M2 of the Metro
Fehérvári út in district XI in the southwestern part of Buda
Lehel tér in district XIII in the north of Pest.

EATING OUT

Note that a 10–15 percent tip, given to the waiter (not left on the table), is customary, unless there is a service charge on the bill.

The price range for a three-course meal for two with a bottle of wine is as follows:

$$$$ = $20 and over
$$$ = $15–$20
$$ = $10–$15
$ = $10 and under

Restaurants in Buda

Alabárdos étterem
Országház utca 2 (On Castle Hill, opposite Mátyás church)
Tel: 356 0851
Mon–Sat noon–4pm, 6pm–midnight
Extensive Hungarian menu, served on Zsolnay porcelain, in an elegant setting. Eat in the medieval building or on outdoor terrace. Best Hungarian wines. $$$$

Aranykaviár
Ostrom utca 19 (M3 to Moskov tér)
Tel: 201 6737
Daily 6pm–midnight
Small, intimate cellar restaurant serving large portions of delicious Russian food. Beluga and Svruga caviar are available, and there's a selection of vodkas. Wine list from the neighbouring Budapest Wine Society. The wall murals and muzak are somewhat disconcerting. $$–$$$

Café Pierrot Restaurant
Fortuna utca 14 (On Castle Hill)
Tel: 375 6971
Daily 11am–1am
Light meals – crêpes are a speciality – served in a cosy interior or on a handful of street tables. After 8pm Café Pierrot features the accompaniment of a wonderful pianist. $$

Kéhli Vendéglő
Mókus utca 22. (HÉV suburban train from Batthyány tér to Arpád híd)
Tel: 250 4241
Mon–Fri 5pm–midnight; Sat, Sun noon–midnight
Housed in a 200-year old building behind the Aquincum Corinthia Hotel, Kéhli Vendéglő enjoys a great reputation. Traditional Hungarian fare is served in a series of small rooms or in a courtyard garden. Freshwater fish and strudels are the specialities. Dinner is accompanied by gypsy music. $$$

Kisbuda Gyöngye étterem
Kenyeres utca 34 (M2 to Batthyány tér)
Tel: 386 6402
Mon–Sat noon–midnight. Reservations recommended
Kisbuda Gyöngye étterem is one of Budapest's most renowned restaurants, not least due to a menu featuring delicious Hungarian dishes. The interior is a salon filled with old furniture in drawing room-style. There are also tables in a pleasant courtyard. Music. $$$–$$$$

Le Jardin de Paris
Fő utca 20 (M3 to Batthyány tér)
Tel: 201 0047
Daily noon–2am
French specialities are graciously served to the accompaniment of a jazz trio in a cosy cellar. Also outdoor dining in a garden area. French and Hungarian wines. **$$$**

Náncsi Néni
Ördögárok út 80 (10-minute walk from bus 56 or tram 56 terminals)
Tel: 397 2742
Daily noon–11pm. Reservations essential Náncsi Néni (Auntie Náncsi) may well be the mother of all home-style Hungarian restaurants. A warm, welcoming atmosphere, gingham tablecloths and home cooking await you at this establishment situated in the Buda hills. Outdoor garden and accordion music. **$**

Önklszolgáló
Hess András tér 4 (second door on left in Fortuna courtyard)
No phone
Mon–Fri 11.30am–2.30pm
Although the dining area is cavernous, Önklszolgáló is a fairly pleasant restaurant that serves enormous, remarkably cheap portions. Self service. **$**

Restaurants in Pest
Articsóka
Zichy Jenö utca 17
Tel: 302 7757
Daily noon–midnight
Articsóka revels in its reputation as *the* place to dine in Budapest, even if its renown owes more to a marvellous decor, atrium and rooftop terrace than to its cuisine, which is best described as Mediterranean with a Hungarian twist. It also has a small theatre for postprandial entertainment. **$$$–$$$$**

Bagolyvár étterem
Állatkerti körút 2 (M1 to Hösök tér)
Tel: 343 0217
Daily noon–11pm
The less expensive sister and neighbour to Gundel. The friendly, all-female staff serve dishes from a limited but excellent menu. Dine indoors or on the terrace. **$$**

Belcanto
Dalszinház utca (8 M1 to Opera)
Tel: 269 2786
Daily, noon–3pm, 6pm–2am
Belcanto, a pleasant Italian restaurant, has an extremely long menu, and its waiters sing operatic arias every night at 10. Open also for buffet lunch. **$$$**

Bombay Palace
Andrássy út 44 (M1 to Octagon)
Tel: 332 8363
Daily noon–2.45pm, 6–11pm.
North Indian cuisine served in quite elegant surroundings. **$$$**

Café Kör
Sas utca 17
Tel: 311 0053
Mon–Sat 10am–10pm
Café Kör, a popular, attractive bistro conveniently situated in the centre of town, serves a range of light meals, many from its extensive vegetarian menu; excellent wine list. **$$**

Fausto's Ristorante
Dohány utca 5
Tel: 269 6806
Mon–Sat noon–3pm, 7–11pm
Italian and international cuisine served in stylish surroundings. **$$$**

Fészek Club
Kertész utca 36 (Tram 4 or 6 to Király utca)
Tel: 322 6043
Daily noon–1am. Reservations essential
A crumbling courtyard illuminated by old-fashioned gas lamps sets the scene for this lovely restaurant, which is especially pleasant on warm summer evenings. A huge choice of Hungarian dishes is complemented by a sign that translates as: 'If you don't find your favourite dish on the menu, we'll make it if we have the ingredients.' **$$**

Gandhi
Vigyázó Ferenc utca 4
Tel: 269 1625
Mon–Sat 10am–11pm.
Vegetarian dishes from around the world. Two daily set menus – the Sun and the Moon plate. Interesting salads. **$**

Left: Hungarian cuisine reflects the country's diverse influences

Gerbeaud Brauhaus
Vörösmarty tér 7
Tel: 429 9000
Daily 9am–11pm
A new eatery in the Gerbeaud Café base-
ment, this spacious, well-furnished beer hall
serves a full menu and beer brewed on the
premises. $$$

Gundel étterem
Állatkerti körút 2 (M1 to Hösök tér)
Tel: 321 3550
Daily noon–4pm, 6.30pm–midnight
Budapest's most famous restaurant. Dine in
an opulent dining room or in a trim garden.
Game and vegetables are Gundel's
specialities. Possibly the most extensive
wine list in city. $$$$

Kádár étkezde
Klauzál tér 9 (M3 to Astoria)
Tel: 321 3622
Tues–Sat 11.30am–3.30pm
Uncle Kádár greets a mixed clientele at this
legendary, atmospheric luncheon room in
the Jewish district. Share a table, enjoy fast
service and a huge portion of Hungarian
food, pay the very modest bill at the front and
be sure to tip the waitress personally. $

Képíró étterem
Képíró utca 3
Tel: 266 0430
Daily noon–2am
Excellent French food is served in a stylish
atmosphere accompanied, on occasions, by
live jazz. The wine list is both unusual and
expensive. $$$$

Lou-Lou Restaurant
Vigyázó Ferenc utca 4 (M1 to Kossuth tér)
Tel: 312 4505
Mon–Fri noon–3pm, 7–11pm; Sat 7–11pm
Romantic, tiny cellar in the financial district.
A long menu (fresh fish a speciality) of
French and modern European cuisine. $$$$

Marquis de Salade
Hajós utca 43 (M2 to Arany János utca)
Tel: 302 4086
Daily 11am–midnight
A remarkable array of vegetarian dishes,
prepared by a range of chefs from countries
such as Italy, China and Russia, are served
in pleasant surroundings. $$$

Múzeum étterem és Kávéháv
Múzeum körút 12
Tel: 267 0375
Mon–Sat noon–1am
In business for over a century. Fish and duck
with fruit are specialities. $$$$

Oroszlános Kút étterem
Vörösmaraty tér 7–8
Tel: 429 9000
Mon–Sat noon–3pm, 6–11pm; Sun noon–
3pm
Attached to the renowned Gerbeaud Café,
which is just around the corner, Oroszlános
Kút is a small, bright and elegant restaurant. On sunny days the light filters through
a glass roof. The cuisine complements the
ambience. $$$$

Papageno
Semmelweis utca 19
Tel: 485 0161
Mon–Fri 11.30am–3pm, 6pm–midnight; Sat
6.30pm–midnight
Small venue for light meals – fine pastas,
exciting entrées and great desserts, plus the
best Hungarian and Italian wines. $$$

Robinson
Városliget tó
Tel: 343 3776
Daily noon–midnight
Built over the City Park lake, this long-
established favourite is informal yet smart.
Hungarian cuisine with roasts cooked on
lava stone. Outdoor terrace; live music. $$$

Above: Gerbeaud's large terrace attracts Budapestik and visitors alike

Sir Lancelot
Podmaniczky utca 14 (Nr Nyugati train station)
Tel: 302 4456
Daily noon–1am. Reservations essential Huge portions served on wooden platters but without cutlery. Waiters dressed in period costume accompanied by appropriate music. You'll love it or loathe it. **$$–$$$**

Szindbád
Markó utca 33
Tel: 332 2966
Mon–Fri noon–3pm, 6pm–midnight; Sat 6pm–midnight
Exclusive softly-lit cellar. Waiters escort diners to the bar, ladies are presented with a complimentary glass of champagne (and are given menus without prices). **$$$$**

Valentine étterem/Várkert casino
Ybl. Miklós tér 9
Tel: 202 4244
Daily 7pm–2am
Elegant establishment in neo-Renaissance building overlooking casino gaming floor and the Danube; innovative menu, fine wine list. **$$$–$$$$**

Vista Café and Restaurant
Paulay Ede utca 7
Tel: 267 8603
Mon–Fri 8am–11pm, Sat, Sun 10am–11pm
Imaginative fare served by friendly staff in large, pleasant space in a travel shop. **$**

Traditional Coffee Houses
Kezét csókolom! This, Budapest's equivalent of the old-fashioned Viennese greeting *küss die Hand, schöne Frau* (kiss your hand, beautiful lady), has survived the political correctness of the past few decades and is still heard in the city's traditional coffee-houses. It could still be the early years of the 20th rather than the 21st century: elegant ladies in fancy hats brandish long cigarette-holders, and gentlemen hidden by their newspapers give the ocasional sign of life with a puff of smoke, all attended by multilingual waitresses. A feature of the city's cafés is the huge selection of cakes and sweets, usually made on the premises, in the display windows. Some of these

Cukrásdza (coffee houses) serve full meals. The following is a list of some of the finest:

Central Café
Károlyi Mihály utca 9
Tel: 266 2110
Mon–Thurs, Sun 8am–midnight; Fri, Sat 8am–1am
One of the city's most famous cafés, recently restored. Dining areas serve full meals.

Lukács Cukrászda
Andrássy út 70
Tel: 302 8747
Mon–Sat 9am–8pm, Sun 10am–8pm.
An exquisite café whose quiet, elegant surroundings constitute the foyer of a bank.

Müvész Kávéház
Andrássy út 29
Tel: 303 5981
Daily 9am–midnight
Popular *fin-de-siècle* café complete with its original fittings. Outdoor terrace.

New York Café and Restaurant
Erzsébet körút 9–11
Tel: 322 3849
Cafe: 10am–midnight
Restaurant: noon–4pm, 6.30pm–midnight
Large, magnificent space in which to eat full meals. A survivor from the *fin de siècle* era, with a wonderfully restored interior.

Ruszwurm
Szentháromság utca 7
Tel: 375 5284
Mon–Fri 10am–7pm: Sat, Sun 10am–8pm
Intimate café, with a couple of outdoor tables, a few steps from Mátyás Church on Castle Hill. Ruszwurm was known in Vienna 100 years ago, and its inexpensive iced coffees and strudels remain popular.

Gerbeaud
Vörösmarty tér 7
Tel: 429 9000
Daily 9am–11pm
An institution since 1858 that retains its fine 19th-century decor. A spacious interior and a large summer terrace attract locals and tourists. Large selection of specialities. Also two Gerbeaud restaurants in the building.

NIGHTLIFE

Budapest enjoys a varied and rich cultural life which most visitors will find to be quite inexpensive. Classical music concerts abound and aficionados of opera and ballet will have plenty of opportunities to sample the local high-culture scene. The season runs mainly from September to May or June; in summer there are three splendid outdoor venues, several churches host regularly excellent concerts, and in July or August the Opera House has a brief summer season.

Operettas and folk music and dancing can be enjoyed on many evenings. Then there is the circus, which performs for 10 months of the year, puppet shows and, of course, concerts by pop stars, local and foreign.

Hungarian-speaking theatregoers will not be disappointed by a lively scene – there are some 30 theatres in the city. It is sometimes possible to catch English-language productions, and several theatres stage big musicals.

Some venues – the Opera House, the Academy of Music, Vígszínház (Merry Theatre) and Pesti Vigadó – are remarkably handsome, and Budapestik observe a decent dress standard when attending concerts and the theatre. Weekly and monthly magazines such as *Budapest in your Pocket* and *Where* carry listings of most events. Most useful of all is the free, Hungarian-language *Pesti-Est*. You can also get relevant information from **Tourinform** *(see Page 88)*.

Venues

Béla Bartók Memorial House
Csalán utca 29
Tel: 394 2100
Venue for chamber music concerts.

Budai Vigadó
Corvin tér 8
Tel: 317 2754
Authentic gypsy music at the home of the Hungarian State Folk Ensemble.

Budapesti Bábszínház (Puppet Theatre)
Andrássy út 69
Tel: 342 2702
Even children who don't speak Hungarian might appreciate productions such as *Little Red Riding Hood* and *Peter and the Wolf*.

Congress Centre
Jagelló út 1–3
Tel: 209 1990
Classical concerts in the largest concert hall in Budapest.

Kolibri Bábszínház (Puppet Theatre)
Jókai tér 10
Tel: 353 4633
Comparable to the Budapesti Bábszínház, this puppet theatre stages timeless classics.

Liszt Memorial Museum
Vörösmarty utca 35
Tel: 322 9804
Venue for chamber music concerts.

Mádach Szinhaz (Mádach Music Theatre)
Erzsébet krt. 29–33
Tel: 478 2000
This excellent company concentrates on big musical productions in a lovingly restored venue.

Mátyás Church
Szentháromság tér 2
Tel: 355 5657
Classical concerts, organ recitals, requiems. While other venues may be closed in summer, the church remains open.

Merlin Theatre
Gerlóczy utca 4
Tel: 317 9338
Plays produced in English and German.

Nagy Cirkusz (Great Circus)
Állatkerti körút 7
Tel: 343 9630
Two performances daily throughout the year except September and October.

Nemzeti Szinhaz (National Theatre)
Hevesi S. tér 4
Tel: 341 3849
A 200-year-old tradition of Hungarian and international dramas and musicals

Operahaz (Opera House)
Andrássy út 22
Tel: 353 0170
The state opera house stages opera and ballet at very reasonable prices.

Right: the internationally acclaimed Chain Bridge serves as a metaphor for unity

Operett Szinház (Operetta Theatre)
Nagymezö utca 19
Tel: 353 2172
Operettas by Franz Lehár and Imre Kalmán, international favourites and big musicals such as *Hello, Dolly*.

Pesti Vigadó
Vigadó tér 2
Tel: 318 9903
Light classical music concerts and kitsch programmes designed for tourists.

Petofi Csarnok
Zichy Mihály út 14 (City Park)
Tel: 251 7266
A good place at which to see contemporary dance performances.

Vígszínház (Merry Theatre)
Szent István körút 14
Tel: 340 4650
Budapest's biggest theatre, restored to its neo-baroque splendour, is home to a company that delights in the big musicals.

Zeneakadémia (Academy of Music)
Liszt Ferenc tér
Tel: 341 4788
The location for classical music, with the best acoustics in the city. Schedules posted at the Kiraly utca entrance to the Academy.

Ticket Agencies
Central Ticket Office
Andrássy út 15
Tel: 267 9737
Mon–Thurs 10am–6pm, Fri 9am–5pm
Opera and classical music concert tickets.

Filharmónia Jegypénztára
Mérleg utca 10
Tel: 318 0281
Mon–Fri 10am–6pm
Tickets for the Philharmonic Orchestra and other classical concerts.

Music Mix
Váci utca 33
Tel: 317 7736
Mon–Fri 10am–6pm, Sat 10am–2pm
The place to get tickets for rock spectaculars and most appearances by visiting pop groups and singers.

Vigadó Ticket Office
Vörösmarty tér 1
Tel: 327 4322
Mon–Fri 9am–7pm, Sat, Sun 10am–3pm
Non-specialist outlet that sells tickets for all types of concert.

Vista Visitor Centre
Paulay Ede utca 7
Tel: 267 8603
Mon–Fri 8am–6pm, Sat, Sun 10am–6pm
An extensive range of tickets for events ranging from classical concerts to diverse sporting events.

Summer Theatres
There are three sizeable open-air summer theatres in Budapest, and each enjoys a reputation for mounting an eclectic range of productions. These include light Rodgers and Hammerstein musicals such as *The King and I*, jazz concerts and, for those wanting a taste of local culture, *Crucified* – a Hungarian Passion play. The theatres are:

Budai Parkszinpad
Kosztolányi Dezsö tér
Tel: 466 9848

Margitszigeti Szabadtéri Színpad
Margaret Island,
Tel: 340 4196

Városmajori Szabadtéri Szinpad
Városmajor
Tel: 267 4844

Cafés

The cafés listed below are not traditional cafés but lively social meeting places which, much like English pubs, tend to serve alcoholic beverages rather than tea and coffee. Most of them serve hot snacks and have piped, or sometimes live, music. The hottest area for café life is Liszt Ference tér (M1 to Oktogon) where you will find the following cafés all in close proximity to each other.

Café Vian
Liszt Ferenc tér 9 (M1 to Oktogon)
Tel: 268 1154
Daily 10am–midnight
Relaxed café with cutting-edge interior that serves 'French bistro food' and attracts a yuppie crowd. Outdoor terrace.

Pesti Est Café
Liszt Ferenc tér (M1 to Oktogon)
Tel: 344 4381
Daily 11am–2am
Pesti Est serves a range of coffees, cocktails and light meals, all accompanied by good music. Outdoor terrace.

Cafe Mediterrán
Liszt Ferenc tér 10 (M1 to Oktogon)
Tel: 344 4615
Mon–Fri 10.30am–12.30am; Sat, Sun 11am–12.30am
Don't be put off by the gaudy orange walls: this is a relaxed, funky and inexpensive spot. Outdoor terrace.

Incognito
Liszt Ferenc tér 3
Tel: 342 1471
Mon–Fri 10am–midnight; Sat, Sun noon–midnight
Upmarket dimly-lit bar featuring jazz-funk and acid-jazz sounds. Outdoor terrace.

Fashion Café
Andrássy út 36
Tel: 311 8060
Mon–Sat 11am–1am; Sun 3pm–1am
Situated around the corner from the cafés listed above, the Fashion Café is the choice drinking spot for the designer-dressed crowd, who doubtless appreciate the wonderful champagne selection.

Angelika
Batthyány tér 7
Tel: 212 3784
Daily 9am–11pm
An impressive setting consists of connecting vaulted rooms in a cavernous interior, with stained-glass windows and marble floors. Also a large outdoor terrace on the Buda bank of the Danube.

Café Miró
Úri u.30
Tel: 375 5458
Daily 9am–midnight
A contemporary affair with a terrace, Café Miró serves light meals and provides subdued live music for a couple of hours in the evenings.

Above: a budding soloist makes his mark in the land of Liszt and Léhar

nightlife

Café Mozart
Erzsébet körút 36
Tel: 352 0664
Mon–Fri 9am–11pm, Sat 9am–midnight, Sun 9am–11pm
The composer after whom Café Mozart is named features throughout this mock-traditional café, which has scenes from Vienna painted on the walls, Mozart's music, and waitresses dressed in 18th-century maid-servant costumes. Great pastries.

Gay Life
For information, call 932 3334, 4–8 pm.

Café Capella
Belgrád rakpart 23 (No.2 tram to Mearcius 15 tér)
Tel: 318 6231
Tues 9pm–4am, Wed–Sun 9pm–5am
Gays and straights turn up for the tacky mid-night drag show: Fri, Sat 11pm and 2am.

Chaos
Dohány utca 38 (M2 to Blaha L.tér or Astoria)
Tel: 344 4884
Daily 9pm–5am
Don't be put off by the art gallery on the ground floor. A long chrome bar in the base-ment leads to a small dance floor. An up-market meeting place for mature males.

Angel
Szövetség utca 33
Tel: 351 6490
Thurs–Sun 10pm–5am
Enormous gay cellar disco.

Bars
Some of the places listed below feature live music, at others the sounds are piped; most serve food.

Club Seven
Akácfa utca 7
Tel: 478 9030
Daily 10am–5am
A classy club which at first glance appears to be a small café, but descend the stairs and you will find rows of tables, a stage for mellow jazz acts and a dance floor. On weekends admission is free for women.

Darshan Café
Krúdy Gyula utca 7 (M3 to Kálvin tér)
Tel: 266 6139
10am till late
A large colourful courtyard at the rear of which is a covered area with a funky bar. There is a full menu and occasional concerts. The Darshan Café also has three shops, one of which has probably the best CD selection in town: the other two are New Age outlets.

Fat Mo's
Nyáary Pál utca 11
Tel: 267 3199
Mon–Sat noon–late, Sun noon–2am
Fat Mo's tends to be packed with a young crowd including numerous foreigners looking for some local love action. Dancing to DJ turntables does not start till after midnight. Food available.

Irish Cat
Meuzeum körút 41 (M3 to Kálvin tér)
Tel: 266 4085
Mon–Fri 11am–2am, Sat, Sun 4pm–2am
Pleasant place for a pub lunch or an evening dinner, with Latin music on Mon, blues on Tues. Guinness on tap.

Old Man's Music Pub
Akácfa utca 13
Tel: 322 7645
Daily 3pm–4am.
A long-popular but ramshackle underground bar and dance floor that attracts the best blues and jazz acts in town. For dinner tables, reservations are essential.

Portside
Dohány utca 7
Tel: 351 8405
Mon–Fri noon–2am; Sat, Sun noon–4am
Basement packed with yuppie singles aiming to pick up a date.

Wall Street-1st Hungarian Alkohol Stock
Andrássy út 19
Tel: 322 7896
Mon–Sat 11am–midnight
A recent addition to the city's nightlife scene, the Wall Street-1st Hungarian Alkohol Stock is an elegant, comfortable bar complete with a separate restaurant.

Casinos

Casino Vigadó
Vigadó utca .2
Tel: 317 0896
Daily 2pm–5am

Las Vegas Casino
Atrium Hyatt Hotel (Roosevelt tér 2)
Tel: 317 6022
Daily 2pm–5am

Grand Casino
Deák Ference utca 13
Tel: 318 9929
Daily 2pm–5am

Várkert Casino
Ybl Miklós tér 9
Tel: 202 4244
Open 2pm–5am

Beer Gardens

Rácz-kert (Serb Garden)
Hadnagy utca 12 (close to the Rác baths)
Tel: 356 1322
Noon till late
A highly popular open-air beer garden that serves good, simple dishes, the Rácz-kert attracts a mature crowd and features amplified music.

Rom-kert
Close to the Rudas baths
A popular open-air beer garden that serves light snacks and attracts a mature crowd. Live music at weekends.

Sörsátor
Városliget (City Park)
Noon–midnight
A large beer tent which is particularly popular with the elderly, especially those who enjoy dancing – waltzes, quicksteps, foxtrots – to a live band that takes the stage at 5pm. Food available.

Zöld Pardon
Petőfi Bridge on Buda side
No phone
Noon–6am
Open-air dance floor that is popular with youngsters. Live music or DJ. Inexpensive drinks plus hot dogs, roasts, grills.

Nightclub

Moulin Rouge
Nagymezö utca 17
Tel: 332 990000
9.30am–3am
A restaurant and café with cabaret and revues. Showtime: 9pm, 11.45pm.

Discos

Bahnhof
Váci út 1 (behind Nyugati train station)
Tel: 302 8599
Thurs–Sat 9pm–4am
Very loud mainstream music blares in one room; crossover in another. Young crowds. No food.

Citadella
Citadella sétány 2
Tel: 209 3291
10pm–4am
The place for young ravers to hit the dance floor while enjoying superlative views of Budapest.

Dokk Backstage
Hajógyári sziget 127 (Obuda)
Tel: 457 1023
Noon–midnight; Fri, Sat disco until 5am
Budapest's nouveau riche hang out in this enormous warehouse on an island in the Danube which has a restaurant, two bars, a gigantic dance floor and great sound system. But it is expensive by Budapest standards. The taxi ride back to city will cost $6.

Nincs Pardon
Almássy tér 11
Tel: 351 4351
8pm–4am
Music and dance on Fri, Sat nights. A wide range of music and mid-30s crowd. Open sandwiches at the bar.

Undergrass
Liszt Ference tér 10
Tel: 343 7611
Tues–Sat 10pm–4am
Funky music in an air-conditioned dance venue beneath the Café Mediterrán. Undergrass attracts a very young crowd and does not serve food. And it's pointless to turn up before midnight.

CALENDAR OF EVENTS

The following is a list of annual events that might appeal to visitors. Public holidays are marked with an asterisk.

January
New Year's Day* (1st): Operetta Gala at the Vigadó.

February
Magyar Filmszemle (first half of month): Hungarian film festival – lasts five days.

March
The Spring Uprising* (15th): a ceremony takes place at the Petőfi Statue outside the National Museum.

Spring festival (mid-Mar): a wide range of cultural events over two weeks. Special exhibitions are mounted in many museums.

April
Easter Sunday/Monday* (or in Mar)
Marathon (last Sunday)

May
Labour Day* (1st)

Book week (last week or possibly first week in June): publishers set up kiosks throughout central Pest to display new titles.

June
Whit Sunday/Monday* (possibly in May)

Búcsú (last weekend): celebration of the departure of Soviet troops from the capital with rock and classical concerts.

Open-Air Theatre Programmes (continues through July and Aug): plays, concerts, ballet, folklore, children's puppet shows in three major locations.

July
Opera and Ballet Festival (late July or early Aug): a 10-day series of operas and ballets at the State Opera House: this is the only opportunity to see a performance in summer.

August
Hungarian Formula 1 Grand Prix (2nd Sunday): the biggest event in Hungary's sporting calendar takes place at Hungaror, 20km (13 miles) east of city.

Traditional Handicraft Fair (middle of month): a three-day event in the Castle District with mostly handmade wares, many of high quality, for sale. Also features craft demonstrations.

St Stephen's Day* (20th): Parades and fireworks over the Danube.

September
National Jewish Festival (early in month or possibly late Aug): a 10-day celebration of all things Jewish.

Budapest International Wine Festival (2nd week): wine tasting, folk and classical musical productions in squares throughout the city.

Sziget Festival (3rd week): held on Obuda island. Said to be Europe's biggest rock and pop festival.

Music Weeks (starts on 25th): the start of a three-week season of classical music and dance performances to mark the anniversary of the death of Béla Bartók.

October
Autumn Festival
Marathon
Remembrance Day* (23rd): a day of mourning to remember the 1956 uprising in which 30,000 were killed and 200,000 fled the country.

December
Mikulás (6th): children leave shoes on window sills for Santa Claus to fill.
Christmas* (25th & 26th)
New Year's Eve (31st): all-night masked ball at the Opera House.

Right: celebrating a national festival

Practical Information

GETTING THERE

By Road

Visitors travelling to Budapest by car will probably drive via Vienna, from where the A4 motorway leads as far as the crossing at Hegyeshalom. From there the M1 motorway runs to Budapest: the first 43km (27 miles) to Gyór is a toll road; the remaining 117km (73 miles) is toll-free. In summer, you are advised to tune in to traffic reports on the radio, as the volume of road users here can be extremely heavy. Alternatively try the Klingenbach/Sopron crossing about 70km (44 miles) to the south of Vienna, or one of the crossings further to the south. If you are driving through Carinthia in Austria, you can cut through Maribor, Slovenia and drive in via Letenye.

If driving you need a valid driving licence and vehicle registration document, plus a car sticker that shows which country you are coming from. The insurance green card is not mandatory, but motoring organisations recommend you bring one, together with special vouchers that can be redeemed if your car needs to be towed home.

By Ship

The Hungarian MAHART company and the Austrian DDSG-Donaureisen company operate hydrofoils and boats that sail between Vienna and Budapest, among other destinations. The trip along the River Danube is picturesque but it is also relatively expensive. In Budapest the ships anchor at Belgrád rakpart, which is located between Erzsébet and Szabadság bridges.

Your local travel agent should be able to furnish you with up-to-date information and schedules; alternatively get in direct touch with DDSG-Donaureisen, Handelskai 265, A-1021 Vienna, tel: 0222-729 2161. Or you could try contacting MAHART, Belgrád rakpart, Budapest V, tel: 318 1704, for the relevant information.

Left: a good way to get around
Right: the national airline

By Plane

Airlines fly to Budapest's Ferihegy airport. The national MALÉV carrier has invested in new planes – 767s for long-haul flights. There are regular flights to and from most European capitals and major cities, several Balkan cities, a number of Middle Eastern cities (Damascus, Tel Aviv, Cairo) and New York. Flight times are as follows:

1hr 10 mins from Berlin
1hr 15 mins from Munich
1hr 50 mins from Amsterdam
1hr 55 mins from Paris
2hr 10 mins from London
2hr 25 mins from Helsinki
2hr 50 mins from Istanbul
10hr 25 minutes from New York

The frequent and comfortable airport minibus will take you to any address. You can buy tickets for the minibus (either single or return) while you wait for your luggage or when you reach the main concourse. To return to the airport on the minibus, call 296 8555 or 296 6283, and the bus will pick you up at any address. For a slower, but cheaper alternative, take bus No 93 to Kőbánya-Kispest Metro station, and then take the M3 Metro line to the city centre. Taxis from the airport are expensive: be sure to check that the meter is running.

A final possibility is to rent a car at the airport, where Hertz and Avis have desks. For good value, however, you will need to shop around. Don't forget to ask if prices include value added tax (VAT) which is currently at a stratospheric 25 percent. *(See Car Rental page 81.)*

By Rail

The main railway line to Budapest from Western Europe runs via Vienna. A dozen trains run daily between the two Danube capitals. Trains from the west, such as the Orient Express, arrive in Budapest at the Keleti pályaudvár, the Eastern Station.

If you are a national requiring a visa, you will require it to board the train. The other long-distance station is the West Station, Nyugati pályaudvár. The third main station in the capital, Déli pályaudvár, is on the Buda side in the western part of the city. From there trains travel to Balaton and to southern Hungary.

To travel from one station to another by road you should allow at least half an hour; less if you take the Metro. For Metro timetable information in German or English, tel: 342 9150.

TRAVEL ESSENTIALS

When to Visit

The best time to visit Budapest is in either the spring or the autumn; summers can be extremely hot and winters can get very cold indeed. At all times, however, there's a lot of cultural activity to enjoy. Bear in mind that in winter pollution resulting from the widespread use of brown coal for heating will asphyxiate the untrained lung.

Passports and Customs

Europeans (except citizens of Albania and Turkey), Americans, nationals of the former Soviet Union, Canadians, Israelis and

Left: a warm welcome

Japanese no longer need to buy a $25 visa before entering Hungary. Most Asians, Middle Easterners and people from Latin America require visas, as do Australians, New Zealanders and Maltese.

No drugs or firearms (unless you are a hunter, in which case you need a special permit from the consulate in your home country) are allowed into the country. CB transmitters and car telephones have to be registered at the border. If you are 16 or older, you are allowed 250 cigarettes, or 50 cigars, or 250 grams of tobacco, two litres of wine and one litre of spirits.

The export of food is limited, but no one seems to check unless you are shifting foodstuffs by the lorry load. However, your wallet may be checked for currency. You are not supposed to take out more than 500 Forint, though sums that are only slightly higher are unlikely to be confiscated.

GETTING ACQUAINTED

The state of Hungary has been in existence for at least 1,000 years; the Parliamentary Republic of Hungary (Magyar Köztársaság) came into being on 23 October 1989, the anniversary of the 1956 uprising.

Since 1989 the government has taken the form of a parliamentary democracy with two chambers. The highest authority in the land is the state president, who has wide-ranging powers under the terms of the constitution, even with regard to the government in power, which is led by a prime minister.

Metropolitan Budapest has 1.9 million inhabitants, roughly a fifth of the country's population. Ethnic minorities – the largest being Serbs, Croats, Slovaks and Romanians – constitute 10 percent of Budapest's population. The city is divided into 22 administrative districts, denoted by Roman numerals. The most important of these are I (Buda) and V (Pest City).

Time

Hungary follows CET (Central European Time). Summertime, when the clocks are put forward one hour, lasts from the final weekend in April until the last weekend in September.

practical information

MONEY MATTERS

The Hungarian currency is the Forint (Ft), or the HUF for Eurocheque purposes. The Forint, which divides up into 100 Fillér, comes in 10,000, 5,000, 1,000, 500 and 200 bills. There are 200, 100, 50, 20, 10, 5, 2 and 1 Fillér coins.

Eurocheques can be cashed in banks and most post offices to a maximum of 30,000Ft. The acceptance of credit cards is spreading rapidly. Cash Machines (ATMs) are widespread, including some convenient outlets at the airport. Exchange rates vary greatly – be wary of disadvantageous deals at railway stations and at some of the exchange offices on Váci utca.

Tipping

Waiters, taxi-drivers, cloakroom and toilet attendants, tour guides and masseurs expect to be tipped. In restaurants a 10 percent tip is expected unless there's a service charge.

GETTING AROUND

Budapest Card/Tickets

The Budapest Card entitles you, plus one child under 15 years of age, to travel on public transport, with free admission to museums and discounts at many baths, shops and restaurants. It can be obtained from tourist offices, travel agencies, hotels, museums as well as main transport ticket offices. Budapest Cards are available for either two or three days' duration.

Single-journey tickets for the Metro, buses and trams can be purchased at stations, many tobacconists, travel offices and vending machines. In addition to single tickets, you can buy books of 10 or 20 tickets, a day card, a three-day card or a one-week card.

The M1 line, which serves the northeast of Pest, travels from Vörösmarty tér all the way to City Park. The terminus is Mexicói út.

The M2 runs west–east, from the South Station (Déli pu) on the Buda side to Batthyány tér (where the suburban railway line HÉV departs for Óbuda and Szentendre), and on to the East Station (Keleti pu) before reaching Örs vezér tér. From there the HÉV travels to Gödöllő and the Hungaroring.

The M3 runs north–south, down the Pest side, from Árpád híd station through the centre of Pest to Kőbánya-Kispest and the airport terminals. All three Metro lines intersect beneath Deák tér in the centre of Pest.

Suburban Railway (HÉV)

Four lines serve Budapest and its immediate environs. Within the city, you can use metro tickets for HÉV travel. For longer journeys, tickets are on sale at the stations.

Buses, Trams and Other Transport

In the city, tickets for buses and trams cost the same as those for the Metro, and they run during the same hours. Night bus lines include the 6É, which follows the 46 tram line on the Nagykörút (Great Boulevard), and the 14É and 50É, which follow the route of the blue Metro (M3). Lines with red numbers are express bus lines, which stop only at important traffic intersections.

There's also the somewhat nostalgic funicular railway (Sikló), which runs up to the castle from the bank of the Danube (daily 7.30am–10pm); the cogwheel railway from Városmajor into the Buda Hills (daily 4.30am–11pm, approx journey time 20-minutes), and the Libegő chairlift to the János-hegy observation point in the eastern part of the city (daily 9am–5pm, journey time 15 minutes).

Taxis

Taxis with illuminated signs are for hire. Alternatively you can call a cab by telephone – most drivers speak some English and German. Taxi drivers are usually quite willing to take passengers on long trips, but make sure you negotiate a price in advance.

Above: heading for a destination near you

As a general rule of thumb, a good car plus driver for a full day costs around $75. The following taxi companies are recommended:

Fötaxi tel: 222 2222
Buda Taxi tel: 233 3333
Tele 5 Taxi tel: 355 5555
6 x 6 Taxi tel: 266 6666
City Taxi tel: 211 1111
Rádió Taxi tel: 377 7777

Public Transport

Buses

Árpád híd Bus Station: Árpád híd, tel: 3299 1450. For buses to the Danube Bend.
Erzsébet tér Bus Station: Erzsébert tér, tel: 317 2562. For western destinations such as Prague and Vienna.
Népstadion Bus Station: Népstadion, tel: 252 1896. For eastern destinations such as Kraków.

Trains

Hungarian Rail (MAV) has an extensive rail network, but it is comparatively expensive.
National Information (daily 6am–9pm): tel: 322 7860.
Sleeping-car reservations can be made at **Utasellato**: tel: 314 0803.
International Information: tel: 342 9150.
MAV customer service office: Apáczdi Csere János utca. 19 (Mon–Fri 9am–5pm), tel: 266 5050 and 266 5753.

Driving

The network of roads in Budapest is of quite a good standard, and the city is served by several sections of motorway.

Information on traffic conditions can be obtained from Utinform: Budapest VI, Andrássy út 11, tel: 322 7052.

The Highway Code is similar to that in the rest of Europe. Note the following:
• **Alcohol** at the wheel is forbidden, as is use of the horn in built-up areas.
• **Seat belts** are compulsory; motor-cyclists must wear helmets.
• **Children** must sit in the back seats.
• **Speed limits**
  50 kph (30 mph) in built-up areas
  80 kph (50 mph) on country roads
  100 kph (60 mph) on trunk roads
  120 kph (75 mph) on motorways.
• **Dimmed Headlights** are mandatory, even during the day, outside built-up areas.

Petrol

Normal (91 octane), Super (98 octane) and lead-free *(ólomentes)* are readily available.

Breakdown Services

The Hungarian Auto Club (Maygar Autóklub) has a 24-hour breakdown service. Call 188. The Auto Club also has an International Aid Service Centre specifically for foreign motorists (tel: 212 2821). The service covers emergency aid, towing and technical advice. Discounts are offered to AA (UK) and AAA (US) members.

Accidents

All accidents should be immediately reported to the police (tel: 107). Insurance claims should be made with Hungária Biztosító, Vadász utca 23–25 (tel: 301 6565).

Above: travel by landau in the northern part of the neighbourhood around the castle

Traffic

Traffic in Budapest tends to be hectic and undisciplined by most Western standards. For information, including help with any difficulties you may encounter on the roads, ring the Hungarian Auto Club's International Aid Service Centre (tel: 212 2821):

For information on roads and conditions call **Útinform** (tel: 332 2238).

For Budapest traffic information call **Főinform** (tel: 317 1173).

Car Rental

To rent a car, you must be able to prove that you are over the age of 21; bring both your national driving licence and your passport to the car-rental office. The rate for an average small car is usually approximately $50 per day, and major credit cards are accepted for car rentals.

It is a good idea to book your car rental in advance, from your home country. This is not only considerably less expensive than making a reservation in Hungary; it is also the most consumer-friendly option. You should bear in mind that the majority of companies represented offer tempting special weekend rates.

The following are all recommended:
Avis: Szervita tér 8, tel: 318 4240; Airport I: 296 6421; Airport II: 296 7265
Budget: Krisztina Körút 41–43 tel: 214 0420; Airport: 296 8197
Hertz: Apáczai Csere János utca 4 tel: 266 4361; Airport 296 0986
Europcar: Üllöi út 60–62 tel: 313 0207; 296 6610.
Inka: Bajcsy-Zsilinszky ut 16, tel: 317 2150.
Fox: Hajogyari sziget 130, tel: 457 1150 (will deliver without charge).

HOURS & HOLIDAYS

Business Hours

Opening times do tend to vary, but in general commercial trading hours (with the exception of groceries and supermarkets) are: Mon–Fri 10am–6pm, Sat 9am–1pm; some shopping centres are also open on Sun, but again times vary.

Budapest's museums are usually open Tues–Sun 10am–6pm. The majority are closed on Mon.

ACCOMMODATION

Hotel rooms can be booked at the airport and at the main railway station. Note that rates are frequently quoted in deutschmarks or in dollars rather than in local currency. Discounts are frequently offered at weekends, in the low season and for relatively long stays.

The room rates for the accommodation options listed below are as follows. All rates are for a double room and include taxes and breakfast:
$ = under $100
$$ = $100–$150
$$$ = $150–$225
$$$$ = over $225

Hotels in Pest
Astoria
Kossuth Lagos utca. 19–21
Tel: 317 3411
Fax: 318 6798
astoria@hungary.net
Astoria occupies a nostalgic old building situated at a busy crossroads. About two-thirds of the 129 rooms retain their original furnishings. **$$$**

Danubius Grand Hotel Margitsziget
Margitsziget (Margaret Island)
Tel: 329 2300
Fax: 329 2589
margotel@hungary.net
An elegant hotel with 164 rooms, connected to its sister hotel (the Thermal) by an underground passage; guests are entitled to free use of the Thermal's facilities. No air-conditioning. **$$**

Right: follow the signs

Hilton West End City Centre
Váci út 1–3
Tel: 288 5500
Fax: 288 5588
info_Budapest-Westend@hilton.com
This 230-room property opened in mid-2000. It is conveniently located next to both the massive West End City Centre shopping mall and the Nyugai station, and it includes all the facilities and luxuries usual in a Hilton. $$$

Hyatt Regency Budapest
Roosevelt tér 2
Tel: 266 1234
Fax: 266 9101
reservation@budapest.hyatt.hu
Situated close to the financial district. Many of its 353 rooms enjoy a river view, but the most striking feature of this eight-floor hotel is the atrium lobby. $$$$

Inter-Continental
Apáczai Csere János utca 12–14
Tel: 327 6333
Fax: 327 6357
budapest@interconti.com
About half of the 398 rooms offer splendid views of the river and, beyond that, the castle district. $$$$

Ibis Centrum
Ráday utca 6
Tel: 215 8585
Fax: 215 8787
A comfortable 126-room property located close to bustling Kálvin tér in central Pest. Three non-smoking floors and a roof garden. Soundproofed windows. $

Kempinski Hotel Corvinus
Erzsébet tér 7–8
Tel: 429 3777
Fax: 429 4777
hotel@kempinski.hu
Budapest's most expensive hotel, with 398 units. Indoor swimming pool. $$$$

King's Hotel
Nagydiófa utca 25–27
Tel/fax: 352 7675
A restored 19th-century building with 79 plain but modern rooms, located in a quiet residential street in the heart of Pest's Jewish district. Some rooms have small balconies overlooking the street. No air conditioning. Strictly kosher. $

Le Meridien
Erzsébet tér 9–10
Tel: 267 4545
Fax: 267 45 53
Opened in 2000, in a former police headquarters, this 218-room central hotel has a swimming pool and all the features expected in Meridien properties. $$$$

Marriott
Apáczai Csere János utca 4
Tel: 266 7000
Fax: 266 5000
marriott.budapest@pronet.hu
Strategically situated between the Erzsébert and Chain bridges. All 362 rooms look over the river and most have balconies. $$$$

Medosz
Jókai tér 9
Tel: 374 3000
Fax: 332-4316
A former trade union hostel which now has 68 simple, clean rooms (no air conditioning), and a restaurant. Located in a quiet area near Andrássy út, the Opera House, and Pest's theatre district. $

Mercure Hotel Budapest Nemzeti
József körút 4
Tel: 477 2000
Fax: 477 2001
nemzeti@pannoniahotels.hu
A handsome, historic hotel that has been restored. Small rooms with high ceilings and

Left: past splendour at the Astoria

spacious bathrooms. Half of the 76 rooms look over a busy street; the other half look onto a lovely interior courtyard. Elegant Art Nouveau restaurant. **$$**

Taverna
Váci utca 29
Tel: 485 3100
Fax: 485 3111
hotel@hoteltaverna.hu
Tour groups tend to dominate this 226-room property located in the heart of Pest's popular pedestrian precinct. **$$**

Thermal Hotel Margitsziget
Margitsziget (Margaret Island)
Tel: 329 2300
Fax: 329 3923
margotel@hungary.net
The big attraction is the spa treatment at this comfortable 206-room (many singles) hotel. All rooms have balcony with views of Margaret Island and the Danube. Guests tend to be elderly. **$$$**

Hotels in Buda
Budapest
Szilágyi Ersébet fasor 47
Tel: 488 9800
Fax: 488 9808
budapesthotel@mail.matav.hu
A towering cylinder whose 289 rooms, especially on the upper floors, have splendid vistas. Refurbished rooms. **$$**

Burg
Szentháromság tér
Tel: 212 0269
Fax: 212 3970
A simple, immaculate 26-room hotel well located on Castle Hill. Rooms have views of Mátyás church. No air conditioning. **$**

Carlton Budapest
Apor Péter utca 3
Tel: 224 0999
Fax: 224 0990
carltonhotel@matavnet.hu
Renamed after extensive renovations, this compact 95-unit hotel (which is part of an Austrian chain) nestles in a cobbled street in Buda's Watertown, below the castle. Small-ish rooms; no restaurant. **$$**

Danubius Hotel Gellért
Szt Gellért tér 1
Tel: 385 2200
Fax: 466 6631
resoff@gellert.hu
The veritable *grande dame* of Budapest hotels, complete with its renowned thermal spa, the Gellért is currently renovating its rooms to bring it into the 21st century. Nearly half of its 233 rooms are singles. Rates include the use of thermal baths. **$$$**

Hilton
Hess András tér 1–3
Tel: 488 6600
Fax: 488 6644
hiltonhu@hungary.net
This landmark building was built on 13th-century ecclesiastical ruins. The Hilton, often said to be Budapest's most desirable hotel, has recently been renovated. Superb views of the Danube and Parliament from about one-third of the 322 rooms. Guests are entitled to use the Thermal Hotel's swimming pool on Margaret Island. **$$$$**

Victoria
Bem rkp 11
Tel: 457 8080
Fax: 457 8088
victoria@victoria.hu
Located in Buda's Watertown district, this property has three floors with nine rooms on each, all with a view of the Danube, from which the hotel is separated by a busy road. No restaurant. **$$**

Pensions
Budapest has about 60 registered pensions (boarding houses), including those listed below. Many are on the outskirts of town in the cool Buda Hills. Rates are approximately $50 for a double room.

Beatrix Panzió
Szehér út 3
Tel: 275 0550
Fax: 394 3730
beatrix@pronet.hu
Pension with 15 rooms. Close to Moskva tér in Buda. Bar, sauna and sundeck. No air conditioning. Guests can enjoy breakfast in the garden in good weather.

Buda Villa Panzió
Kiss áron utca6
Tel: 275 0091
Fax: 275 0092
budapans@mail.datanet.hu
This comfortable, 10-room pension is located in the hills above Moskova tér. There is a bar and a delightful small garden, but no air conditioning.

City Panzió Pilvax
Pilvas köz 1–3
Tel: 266 7660
Fax: 317 6396
pilvax@taverna.hu
Opened in 1997, this pension is relatively quiet, despite its location in the heart of Pest. The 32 rooms come equipped with electric fans. No restaurant.

Radio Inn
Benczúr utca 19
Tel: 322 8284
Situated on a leafy avenue in the embassy district of Pest, Radio Inn features a pleasant garden in addition to its 32 immaculate, large apartments, each complete with kitchen and TV.

Hostels and Private Rooms

A number of local householders with rooms to rent invariably meet trains arriving at Keleti station. The private rooms they offer are not registered with any authority, so there's no guarantee of quality – you could be pleasantly surprised, or you could live to regret taking what is bound to be a gamble. Cut the risk by booking a registered private room through a tourist agency.

Also located at Keleti station is an office for youth hostels (7am–10 or 11pm). Hostel and student cards are not required in Budapest hostels.

Caterina Youth Hostel
Andrássy út 47 (doorbell No.11)
Tel: 342 0804
Fax: 352 6147
Caterina has one 18-bed dormitory, one bedroom that sleeps four, and two two-bed rooms. All are very clean, and there is no curfew, but you must be out between 10am and noon to permit cleaning. **$6–$15**.

Citadella Hostel
Citadella sétány
Tel: 466 5794
Fax: 386 0505
Wonderful eagle-eye views from 10- and 12-bed dormitories. No curfew imposed but the location is awkward to reach. Friendly, helpful staff. Dorm beds **$6**.

Station Guesthouse
Mexikói út 36/b
Tel: 221 8864
Fax: 383 4034
station@mail.matav.hu
It's always party-time at the Station. Mixed-sex dormitories (four to eight beds), and a well-stocked 24-hour bar and pool table. Live music twice a week. Fully equipped kitchen and internet access. **$6–$12**.

Charles Apartment House
Hegyalja út 23
Tel: 201 1796
Fax: 202 2984
The Charles features 22 apartments in one building in Buda plus additional apartments nearby. The accommodation is clean but somewhat small; all flats have bathroom and kitchen. Reception open 24 hours. Neighbouring tennis court. **$45–$55**.

City Centre Apartments,
Thokoly út 16, opposite Keleti train station
Tel: 416 2342
ccity@mail.datanet.hu
A choice of spotless four-, three- and two-bed apartments near the city centre, plus rooms in the proprietor's home. **$10–$30**.

Camping
Romai Camping
1031 Szentendrei út 189
Tel: 388 7167
Grounds for 2,500 campers on the road to Szentendre (20 minutes on HÉV). The 45 cabins are open from mid-Apr–mid-Oct. Use of nearby swimming pool.

Zugligeti "Niche" Camping
1121 Zugligeti út 101
Tel: 200 8346
Buda woods site at the 158 bus terminal with room for 260 campers. Good restaurant.

The following pharmacies are open around the clock.
II, Frankel Leó út 22, tel: 212 4406
III, Vörösvári út, tel: 84 368 6430
IV, Pozsonyi utca. 19, tel: 379 3008
VI, Teréz körút. 41, tel: 311 4439
VIII, Rákóczi út 39, tel: 314 3695
IX, Üllői út 121, tel: 220 8947
X, Liget tér, tel: 3 260 6334
XII, Alkotás utca. 1/B, tel: 355 4691

Emergency Numbers
The following emergency services numbers can be dialled from any telephone:
Ambulance: 104
Fire Brigade: 105
Police: 107

HEALTH & EMERGENCIES

Doctors
First aid and doctors' visits have to be paid for by the patient, usually in foreign currency. Private medical attention is available at the following clinics:

International Medical Services
Váci út 202
Tel: 329 9349
Mon–Fri 7.30am–8pm
and at Vihar utca 29 (in Obuda)
Tel: 250 1899
24-hours

American Clinic
Hattyú utca 14 (5th floor)
Tel: 224 9090
Mon–Thurs 8.30am–7pm, Fri 8.30am–6pm, Sat 8.30am–noon, Sun 10am–2pm

24-Hour Dentists

SOS Dental Service
Király utca 14
Tel: 269 6010

Falck SOS Hungary
Japy utca 49/b
Tel: 200 0100

Pharmacies (Gyógyszertár)
You need a doctor's prescription for virtually all medicine, and payment must be made in cash. Normal pharmacy opening hours are Mon–Fri 8am–8pm, Sat 8am–2pm.

COMMUNICATIONS & NEWS

Post
The city's main post office at Petőfi Sándor utca. 13–15 is open Mon–Fri 8am–8pm, Sat 8am–2pm.

The post office near the Keleti railway station (Baross tér 11/c) is open Mon–Sat 7am–9pm.

The post office near the Nyugati railway station (Térez körút. 51–53) is open Mon–Sat 7am–9pm, Sun 8am–8pm.

Important Phone Numbers:
Directory enquiries (domestic): 198
Directory enquiries (international): 199
Wake-up service: 193

Telephone
Public phones are operated by 10-, 20-, 50- and 100-forint coins. Alternatively you can use phone cards, which cost 800 or 1800 forints, and are available from newsstands, tobacconists, post offices and hotels.

For calls abroad, dial 00, followed by:
Australia (61)
Canada and United States (1)
Germany (49)
Italy (39)
Japan (81)
The Netherlands (31)
Spain (34)
UK (44).

Above: city symbols take pride of place on the police crest

US phone card numbers are as follows:
AT&T 00-360111
MCI 00-800 01411
Sprint 00-800 01877

Cybercafés

Ami
Váci utca 40
Tel: 267 1644
Open 24 hours. 50 terminals.

Vista Internet Café
Paulay Ede utca 7
Tel: 267 8603
Weekdays 8am–10pm Weekends 10am–
10pm. Eight terminals.

Teleport Internet Café
Vas utca 7 (M3 to Blaha Lujza tér)
Tel: 267 6361
Mon–Sat noon–10pm. 12 terminals.

Mátav Internet Café
*Petőfi Sándor 17–19 (Belvárosi Telephone
Centre)*
Tel: 267 6618
Weekdays 9am–8pm, weekends 10am–3pm.
16 terminals.

Budapest Net
Kecskeméti utca 5
Tel: 328 0292
Daily 10am–10pm. 30 terminals.

Plaza Internet Club
DunaPlaz Shopping Mall
Váci út 178
Tel: 465 1126
Daily 10am–10pm. 16 terminals.

Easynet
Váci út 19-21 (in alley to Millenium Centre)
Tel: 485 0460
Daily 9am–10pm. 16 terminals.

MEDIA

The best source of tourist information is the
bimonthly, English-language *Budapest in
Your Pocket* magazine. Hotel receptions and
tourist agencies stock monthlies such as
Where, which have lots of advertising. Street
vendors and large hotels sell international
newspapers and magazines.

The Petőfi FM radio station broadcasts
daily news in German and English at noon.
Satellite TV carries international programmes and news in English and German.

LANGUAGE

Hungarian belongs to the Finno-Ugric
family of languages. Its only relations in
Europe are Finnish and Estonian, though
Hungarians and Finns would not understand
each other. A few old words excepted (*vaj*
for butter), only linguists can link the two.

In Hungarian, the emphasis is always on
the first syllable – the accent on, say,
Andrássy, is not a stress mark; it serves only
to lengthen the vowel slightly.

a = a as in car
á = open a as in after
c = ts
e = e as in especially
é = a as in bare (the distinction between
e and the long é is very important: *segg*
means bottom, and *ség*, see the salutation
below, is a common suffix: eg. *hidegség*
means cold, *hidegseg* means cold bottom).
gy = a run-together dyuh
i = short ee
í = long ee
ly = long i with a sound, a kind of yuh
ny = a kind of nyuh
ty = an aspirated tyuh (tyuk = tee-ook)
o = short o as in horror
ó = long o as in Poland
ö = e as in perfect
ő = same as ö but longer

Above: no Hungarian is needed to understand these signs

s = sh
sz = s
u = oo
ú = oooo
ü = as in German, or u in French
fl = as ü but longer
zs = as in Zsa Zsa Gabor

The language is agglutinative, which means two things. First you stick prepositions, personal articles, and a variety of case suffixes at the end of the word. The result is, for example, 'Health our to!' (*Egészségünkre!*).

Like the Germans, Hungarians join words together with lengthy results: *fagylaltkülönlegességek*, for example, means ice-cream specialities. Verbs, on the other hand, come apart, but not with Germanic regularity. Among the strangest floating particles is *meg*, which indicates a completed action. Unfortunately, this complexity allows little room for pidgin Hungarian – the juxtaposition of undeclined verbs and nouns gives no meaning.

The Akadémiai Kiadó is the publisher of a small but very useful Hungarian-English dictionary that you can find in most of the larger bookstores in Budapest.

Common Words and Phrases

Yes	*Igen*
No	*Nem*
Pardon	*Bocsánat*
Excuse me	*Elnézést*
Good morning	*Jó reggelt kívánok*
Good day	*Jó napot kívánok*
Good evening	*Jó estét kívánok*
Good night	*Jó éjszakát kívánok*
Goodbye	*Viszontlátásra*
(colloquially	*visz'lát*)
Bon appétit	*Jó étvágyat kívánok*
Please	*kérem szépen*
Thank you	*köszönöm szépen*
How much is it?	*Mennyibe kerül?*
Is there... ?	*Van... ?*
I'd like to pay	*fizetni (kérem)*
Where is... ?	*Hol... ?*
Left	*balra*
Right	*jobbra*
Straight	*egyenesen*
Naturally	*persze*
Hotel	*hotel, szálloda*
Double room	*kétágyás szoba*
Single room	*egyágyás szoba*

Bathroom	*Fürdöszoba*
Toilet	*WC, toalett, mosdó*
Shop	*bolt, üzlet*
Price	*ár*
Closed	*zárva*
Open	*nyítva*
Help	*segítség!*
Doctor	*orvos*
Ambulance	*Mentőauto*
Police	*rendőrség*
Leave me alone	*Hagyj békén*
	(fairly polite)

Tessék is universally applied and can mean 'please' (inviting you to help yourself); it is also a way to answer a telephone, and a waiter is likely to approach you with the words *tessék parancsolni* (please, order). It can also mean 'there you go', as in proving a point.

Numbers

one *Egy*
two *kettő*
three *három*
four *négy*
five *öt*
six *hat*
seven *hét*
eight nyolc
nine kilenc
ten tíz
11 tizenegy
12 tizenkettő
20 húsz
30 harminc
40 negyven
50 ötven
60 hatvan
70 hetven
80 nyolcvan
90 kilencven
100 szász
1.000 ezer

Days (Mon–Sun): *hétfő, kedd, szerda, csütörtök, péntek, szombat, vásárnap.*

SPORT & LEISURE

Bowling: Vilati Bowling Centrum, Duna Plaza Mall, Váci út 178, tel: 465 1555.
Squash: City Squash Club, II, Marzibányi tér 13, tel: 335 2518.

practical information

Riding: National Riding School, VIII, Kerepesij út 7, tel: 313 5210. Petneházy Country Club, II, Feketefej utca 2–4, tel: 376 5992.

Tennis: Hungarian Tennis Association, XIV, Dózsa György út 1–3, tel: 252 6687.

This organisation holds a comprehensive list of clubs and courts.

Films and Photography

Films and cassettes of all the major brands are inexpensive in Hungary. It's not hard to find same-day (often within an hour) processing. Try **Fotex** (Váci utca 9 and other locations) or **Fuji Film** (Dévia u. 26–28).

USEFUL ADDRESSES

Tourist Offices

Ibusz, Hungary's long-standing travel agency, is now privatised. It has offices in many cities in the world, including:

London: Hungarian National Tourist Office, 46 Eaton Place, London SW1X 8AL, tel: 020 7823 1032.

New York: Hungarian Tourist Office, 150 East 58th Street, New York 10155-3398, tel: (212) 355 0240.

Tourist offices make hotel reservations and change money, but don't always carry up-to-date brochures. Many expensive hotels have a tourist office in the lobby. A useful office is the international Tourist Information Service **Tourinform** in Budapest, Sütő utca 2, off Deák tér, tel: 317 9800. Alternative sources of information are as follows:

Budapest Tourist
Roosevelt tér 5
tel: 317 3555.

Ibusz
Ferenciek tere 10
tel: 318 6866

Vista Visitor Centre
Paulay Ede u. 7
tel: 268 8888
(an excellent travel shop and restaurant).

Foreign Embassies in Budapest

Austria
VI, Benczúr u. 16, tel: 351 6700.

Australia
XII, Királyhágó tér 8–9, tel: 201 8899.

Canada
XII, Budakeszi út 32, tel: 275 1200

Germany
XIV, Stefánia út 101–103, tel: 467 3500.

Great Britain
V, Harmincad utca 6, tel: 266 2888.

United States
V, Szabadság tér 12, tel: 267 4400.

MALÉV Offices Abroad

MALÉV, the national airline, has a number of offices worldwide, including the following:

Canada: Toronto, tel: (416) 944-0093.

Israel: Tel Aviv, tel: (972 3) 524 6171.

UK: London, tel: (020) 7439 0577.

US: New York, tel: (212) 757 6480, toll free: (800) 223 6884;

Chicago, tel: (312) 819 5353

Los Angeles, tel: (310) 286 7980.

Airline Offices in Budapest

In Hungary, it is customary to contact a travel agency when you wish to book a flight rather than contact an airline directly. However, to reconfirm a return flight you should telephone the airline.

MALÉV
Airport office – tel: 296 9696.

Air France
Krisztóf tér 5
tel: 318 0411

Austrian Airlines
Régiposta utca 5,
tel: 327 9080.

British Airways
Rákóczi utca 1–3,
tel: 318 3299.

British Midland
Váci utca 19–21,
tel: 266 8435/6.

Lufthansa
Váci utca 19,
tel: 266 4511.

Swissair
Krisztóf tér 7–8,
tel: 328 5000.

Flight information in Budapest
Departure Information, tel: 296 7000.
Arrival Information, tel: 296 8000.

Lost and Found
Ring the appropriate number listed below:

Public Transport
BKV, Akácfa utca 18, tel: 322 6613.

Railway stations and trains
Keleti pu (East), tel: 322 5615
Nyugati pu (West), tel: 349 0115
Déli pu (South), tel: 375 9485.

On the street
Central Police Commissariat, Deák Ferenc
utca 16–18, tel: 318 0080.

Travellers' cheques and credit cards
Hungarian National Bank, tel: 353 260.

FURTHER READING

Nonfiction

Apa Publications, *Insight Guide Hungary*
(3rd edition). A full guide to the history, culture and sights of the country.
Apa Publications, *Insight Guide to Budapest*.
(3rd edition). Comprehensive guide to the
history, culture and sights of the city.
George Lang, *Cuisine of Hungary* (Penguin).
All you need to know about Hungarian food.
Stephen Kirkland, *The Wine and Vines of
Hungary* (New World Publishing, Budapest).
Thorough coverage of the country's wines
and winemakers.
John Lukács, *Budapest* (Weidenfeld). Highly
informative account of politics and society
in Budapest at the turn of the 20th century.
Robert Bideleux, Jan Jeffries, *A History of
Eastern Europe: Crisis and Change* (Rout-
ledge). Excellent wide-ranging history.
A.J.P. Taylor *The Habsburg Monarchy,
1809–1918* (Hamish Hamilton). A leading
British historian's analysis of the final
century of the Austro-Hungarian empire.
Judit Frigyesi, *Béla Bartók and Turn-of-the-
Century*. (University of California Press).
Very readable book about intellectual life
in Budapest around 1900.
Michael Stewart, *The Time of the Gypsies*
(Westview Press). Superb account of the life
of gypsy communities in Hungary.
Giorgio and Nicola Pressburger, *Homage to
the Eighth District* (Readers International).
Poignant short stories about Jewish life in
Budapest before, during and after the Holo-
caust by twins who fled Hungary in 1956.
Erno Szép, *The Smell of Humans* (Arrow).
Harrowing recollections of the Holocaust
in Hungary.
Patrick Leigh Fermor, *A Time of Gifts* and *Be-
tween the Woods and the Water* (Penguin).
Classic books by a renowned English travel
writer. The first is about a walk across Europe
which concludes in Hungary. The second is
about the Great Plains and Transylvania.

Fiction

Peter Esterházy, *Helping Verbs of the Heart*
(Weidenfeld & Nicolson). A tense tale that
centres on a son's grief following the death
of his parents.
Peter Nadas, *A Book of Memories* (Vintage).
Brilliant contemporary novel by Hungarian
author.
Zsigmond Móricz, *Be Faithful Unto Death*
(Penguin). Novel by the late 19th-century
Hungarian author reveals how the country's
people see themselves.
Gyula Krúday, *Adventures of Sinbad* (Ran-
dom House). Stories about a gourmand and
womaniser: quite possibly autobiographical.

Right: a ready smile, even in winter

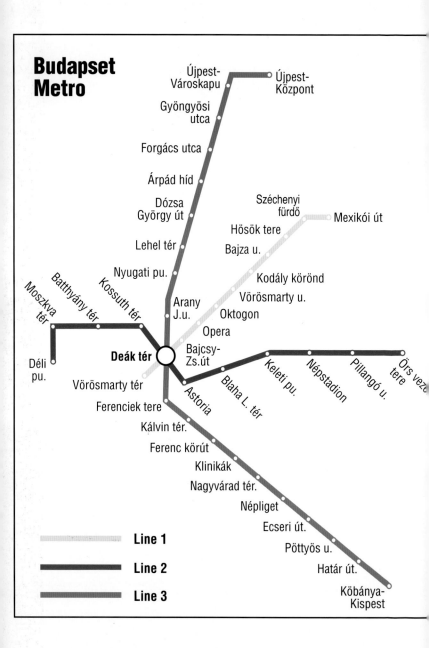

Budapset Metro

Line 1

Line 2

Line 3

ACKNOWLEDGEMENTS

1, 5, 8/9, 27t, 39t, 40, 43, 46, 47, 53, 54, 55, 57t & b, 58t & b, 59, 60, 61, 65, 80, 86	**Marcus Brooke**
24, 63	**Alfred Horn**
12, 13, 15	**Hans-Horst Skuppy**
2/3, 34b, 41, 56, 75, 78, 81, 85	**Hansjörg Künzel**
77	**MALEV Airline**
22, 25t, 28t & b, 29, 37, 48, 52t & b, 66, 72	**Marton Radkai**
20, 21, 23, 25b, 26, 27b, 29, 31t & b, 32t & b, 33, 34t, 35, 36t & b, 38, 39b, 44, 45, 50t & b, 51, 62, 68, 71, 76, 79, 89	**Mark Read**
16	**Janos Stekovics**
Cover	**Oliver Benn/Stone**
Back Cover	**Mark Read**
Cover Design	**Carlotta Junger**
Cartography	**Berndtson & Berndtson/Maria Donnelly**

© APA Publications GmbH & Co. Verlag KG Singapore Branch, Singapore

INSIGHT
Pocket Guides

Insight Pocket Guides pioneered a new approach to guidebooks, introducing the concept of the authors as "local hosts" who would provide readers with personal recommendations, just as they would give honest advice to a friend who came to stay. They also included a full-size pull-out map. Now, to cope with the needs of the 21st century, new editions in this growing series are being given a new look to make them more practical to use, and restaurant and hotel listings have been greatly expanded.

Also from Insight Guides...

Insight Guides is the classic series, providing the complete picture with expert and informative text and stunning photography. Each book is an ideal travel planner, a reliable on-the-spot companion – and a superb visual souvenir of a trip. 193 titles.

Insight Maps are designed to complement the guidebooks. They provide full mapping of major destinations, and their laminated finish gives them ease of use and durability. 100 titles.

Insight Compact Guides are handy reference books, modestly priced yet comprehensive. The text, pictures and maps are all cross-referenced, making them ideal books to consult while seeing the sights. 127 titles.

INSIGHT POCKET GUIDE TITLES

Aegean Islands	Canton	Israel	Nepal	Sikkim
Algarve	Cape Town	Istanbul	New Delhi	Singapore
Alsace	Chiang Mai	Jakarta	New Orleans	Southeast England
Amsterdam	Chicago	Jamaica	New York City	Southern Spain
Athens	Corfu	Kathmandu Bikes	New Zealand	Sri Lanka
Atlanta	Corsica	& Hikes	Oslo and Bergen	Stockholm
Bahamas	Costa Blanca	Kenya	Paris	Switzerland
Baja Peninsula	Costa Brava	Kraków	Penang	Sydney
Bali	Costa del Sol	Kuala Lumpur	Perth	Tenerife
Bali Bird Walks	Costa Rica	Lisbon	Phuket	Thailand
Bangkok	Crete	Loire Valley	Prague	Tibet
Barbados	Croatia	London	Provence	Toronto
Barcelona	Denmark	Los Angeles	Puerto Rico	Tunisia
Bavaria	Dubai	Macau	Quebec	Turkish Coast
Beijing	Fiji Islands	Madrid	Rhodes	Tuscany
Berlin	Florence	Malacca	Rome	Venice
Bermuda	Florida	Maldives	Sabah	Vienna
Bhutan	Florida Keys	Mallorca	St. Petersburg	Vietnam
Boston	French Riviera	Malta	San Diego	Yogjakarta
Brisbane & the	(Côte d'Azur)	Manila	San Francisco	Yucatán Peninsula
Gold Coast	Gran Canaria	Melbourne	Sarawak	
British Columbia	Hawaii	Mexico City	Sardinia	
Brittany	Hong Kong	Miami	Scotland	
Brussels	Hungary	Montreal	Seville, Cordoba &	
Budapest	Ibiza	Morocco	Granada	
California,	Ireland	Moscow	Seychelles	
Northern	Ireland's Southwest	Munich	Sicily	

INDEX